Modern Speed Reading

Learn to Inhale and Absorb Written
Content and Improve Speed, Retention,
and Comprehension

Jimmy McMaster

Table of Contents

Introduction

Reading has been the litmus test for success for centuries. Literacy in the Middle Ages was a skill limited to priests, monks, and scribes. The development of Western civilization since then has progressed greatly as literacy has spread. Those who can read and write have had an advantage and greater social standing than those who can't or those who read poorly.

The 20th century saw vast increases in worldwide literacy, but as we head for the middle of the 21st century, we have also increased the amount of information that every person needs to wade through. Being able to read and understand all the information that is thrown at us is more important than ever.

Reading efficiently and effectively has a direct bearing on how successful we are and even how successful our pursuit of happiness ultimately is. Studies have shown a correlation between how much people read and how happy they rate themselves. Therefore, it is only logical that the faster one reads, the more reading one can do and the better their chances are for being successful and happy.

Speed Reading: Urban Legend?

Speed reading, if you're not familiar with it, may seem to be too good to be true. Most people may have heard of various commercial programs, such as the Evelyn Wood Reading Dynamics program. If you're old enough, you might remember TV ads or advertisements in the Sunday papers. Infomercials always raise suspicion—they must be a scam, right?

Not necessarily. Sure, there are programs that are more interested in making money than delivering what they promise, and that gives the topic a bad name. But the truth is that there are numerous people who have been known to be very fast readers, and it has helped them be successful.

President Kennedy was known to be a very fast reader. He sent members of his staff for training in speed reading to help process large amounts of intelligence and keep the country briefed. Remember, the Cuban missile crisis occurred years before search engines or the internet existed, so it was hard work writing and reading memos and briefs, and it took a lot of time. Anything to speed the process up without sacrificing quality was worthwhile. Presidents Nixon and Carter also continued this tradition at the White House (Vanderlinde, 2018).

Part of understanding the truth of what speed reading is means understanding what it really involves. People can certainly increase the speed at which they read. Being able to scan a phone book and memorize it in five minutes is a parlor trick and not what anyone should expect to be able to do when it comes to speed reading.

Speed reading is *not* the same as skimming, and it is *not* cheating. It really is just a collection of techniques that allow a person to read every word more efficiently and without wasted effort. Some people are able to speed read faster than others just as some people naturally read faster than others. What it comes down to is optimizing the reading process for each individual. If you're going to do anything, why not do it to the best of your abilities? Reading is no exception.

Speed reading definitely has benefits, but it is not a magic bullet. You will save time in the future, but you have to invest a significant amount of time in training to read quickly. You are not going to have instant results. This may be why some people think speed reading is not a "real thing," but that's a case of unreasonable expectations. You wouldn't expect to go to a gym two Saturdays in a row and come out looking like a bodybuilder. Training for speed reading is more like bodybuilding for your mind.

Benefits & Expectations

The many benefits of speed reading are hard to deny. How much time do you spend reading during your day, whether it's emails, texts, documents, or sitting down with a good book? The average person is spending more time reading every day, even if less of that time is spent reading for pleasure. Americans spend about five hours per day reading email (three hours for work, two hours for personal email), but only an average of 16 minutes reading for pleasure (Wylie, 2021). Five hours! That's nuts! If you could shave an hour off of that every day, it would be a remarkable improvement.

In addition to having more time to devote to other interests, you can improve your comprehension and understanding, even your vocabulary and memory. This is not witchcraft. It's actually because spending time working on those skills contributes to your reading speed. You will see those results because you intentionally work toward them.

Anything you do that works on memory, vocabulary, and other mental faculties is going to improve your mental flexibility. All of these are part of improving speed reading. For that matter, reading has even been shown to reduce the risk of developing Alzheimer's disease (*Keep Reading*, 2014).

It is true that you will have to put in your time "in the woodshed" to get good at speed reading. You won't master it overnight. You will have to spend a lot of time training, developing habits, and working at it. But that's not to say that you will have to wait years before you get *any* reward. You will start to see results in a few days or weeks, but it's when you compare your reading speed after, say, a year to when you first started that you will be pleasantly surprised.

This book is arranged to present explanations of the different aspects of reading in the first few chapters. Understanding *how* things work is important so you can make changes in a methodical and productive manner. Chapter 9 is where you will find more practical exercises and suggestions.

It is not necessary to *completely* read the first part of this book before trying things. You will get the most benefit by understanding things first, but speed reading isn't a skill you can learn by osmosis. You have to practice, so don't be afraid to try things from Chapter 9 before you get there.

This book isn't intended to be a complete speed reading course, but it is intended to give you a number of tools and some of the understanding you need to teach yourself to read faster. Ultimately, *you* are the one in charge. If you jump into Chapter 9 and completely ignore the rest of the book, it isn't going to do you any harm, but you won't get the full value out of the exercises.

This means that if you don't see the progress you want fast enough, don't blame the book—and don't get down on yourself either. Keep at it, and hopefully these are methods that will work for you. The other side of that coin is that if you make great strides, you also can't give this book all the credit for your success.

So best of luck in your new speed reading adventure. On your (book)marks, get set, go!

Chapter 1:
Reading, the Brain, and the Body

Disclaimers

Speed reading is a powerful tool. It can help you get to the root of problems more quickly and solve them with the benefit of having more information at your disposal, and it can open doors and reduce stress in your personal and professional life. But before we go any further, let's take a minute and be clear about why it's not a magic bullet and why the results will vary from one person to another.

The first thing is that we have to acknowledge that not everybody's brain is wired the same way. Some people are more visually oriented and others are more verbally oriented, for example. There is a broad range of abilities, even without getting into the terms that are currently accepted: "neurotypical" and "neurodivergent."

Some people might double from reading 200 words per minute to 400 words per minute, while others might only improve to 250 words per minute by using the concepts in this book. Remember, the person who goes from 50 words a minute to 200 words a minute has made twice the improvement of someone who goes from 200 to 400. What's important is that you are improving, and the only person you need to compete with is yourself.

Additionally, we are assuming, without judgment, that you have normal or correctable vision. Some of the aspects of speed reading encourage making use of peripheral vision, for instance, but people who have problems with peripheral vision may find this challenging. This is not to say that speed reading requires perfect vision—far from it!

Developing specialized techniques to help each person cope with their own visual challenges is beyond the scope of this book, though. I would encourage you to see if you can adapt or make use of as many techniques as you can, and if there are some that you can adapt in a way that works for you, then that's excellent. Again, remember that if you make a small improvement, that's still an improvement.

Finally, this book is trying to help you reach your potential for reading. Speed reading is not a trick to learn to make it into a record book. If you are going to try for a record, the one you should be looking for is a personal best, and don't worry about anybody else. It's rude to read over someone else's shoulder!

Reading Is Both Mental and Physical

With those thoughts in mind, let's turn to the topic of reading. When was the last time you gave the practice of reading any thought? Odds are that it's been many, many years. Reading is something most of us take for granted. We learn it when we're young, so we assume that we've mastered it. It turns out that there's a difference between being competent at something and excelling at it. Unfortunately, school, work, and daily life only teach us to read until we're competent. You have to push further to excel.

So to take a fresh look at this skill called reading, you should start by recognizing that there are two parts to it: the physical side and the mental side. There are things you can do to improve the way you approach reading on both fronts.

The physical movements of your eyes are not very big, nor are they something most people have ever thought about. Consider the small adjustments your eyes have to make to read a line of text. Some are tiny, like moving from one word to the next, and others are bigger, like jumping back to the beginning of the next line or moving to the top of the next page.

You start to see that there's a lot going on here. Let's say that you move your eyes six times while reading a single line. Now multiply that by the number of lines on a page (between 30 and 50), so that's about 200–300 movements per page. If your book has 200 pages, that's 40,000–60,000 movements!

If you could reduce how much you have to move your eyes, it would speed things up. Similarly, even though the movements are small, you want them to be as efficient as possible, and you can make improvements in both of these areas.

You may not think about it, but your hands come into play when you're reading. Holding the book comfortably and turning the pages efficiently are other areas where you can make an organized effort to increase your speed. Not only that, but if the physical movements of your hands and eyes are more practiced, you also free your brain up to do more processing, so the gains are multiplied. This is important because your brain is involved in every movement—no matter how tiny—your eyes and hands make.

What Your Brain Does With Information

The mental side of reading is pretty amazing, when you stop to think about it. Science still doesn't have a good understanding of exactly *how* the brain processes certain signals, but there are good answers to the question of *what* processes occur.

First, your eyes turn the symbols you see on the page into electrical signals that enter your brain. The signals representing those symbols have to be decoded and matched with sounds you know. For most people, those sounds have to be processed to make words, then the words are put together to make sentences. At a higher level, you are making inferences, which is when you connect the ideas you are acquiring to other information you already know in order to make sense of them (Kendeou et al., 2014).

All those steps seem to be a straightforward path to comprehending what we read, but there's a bit more to it than that. There is another level of management, called executive function, that helps control our behavior while engaged in performing a task. There are two types of executive function employed in reading: working memory and inhibition (Kendeou et al., 2014).

Working memory is the short-term memory that holds onto information while you are processing it and making inferences. Children have not developed the same level of executive function as adults, but reading skills are not taught to take advantage of the extra capacity that we develop as we mature. This gives us room to harness some of our undeveloped potential.

Inhibition is the executive function that weeds out the good information from the bad. It "inhibits" us from remembering false information. (Not to be confused with the kind of inhibition that keeps us from running out into the street naked.) In a sense, inhibition is what keeps our minds focused and not wandering off into whatever daydreams a certain word or phrase might evoke. There are times when that's the appropriate thing to do—like when reading abstract images in poetry—and times when it's not.

Attention is also a key part of being able to read. Attention span is, again, something that continues to develop long after it has been declared that we're "finished" learning to read. The ability to focus selectively and efficiently, ignoring distractions, is a necessary part of reading. The joke that people always want us for something as soon as we pick up a book is funny because we all know instinctively that reading takes concentration.

In order to pay attention, we have to be able to adapt our processing to the task at hand. This is the first time, but certainly not the last, that you will hear the advice to do *one* thing at a time in this book. Do not try to multitask. If you aren't giving reading your full attention, you're not doing it as well as you could be. The better you keep your attention on your reading, the better you read.

To sum up, your brain is controlling the movements your body makes while reading as well as processing visual input as you use memory, recognition, language centers to extract information, and executive functions to keep it all going while separating the wheat from the chaff. That's quite a workload, and anything that will help streamline it will pay dividends.

Retaining Information

Now that you have seen how much investment you have to make in order to read anything, it would be a real shame to have to redo it because you didn't remember what you read. This is where we move from the short-term working memory to the long-term memory that is used to retain what we read long after we put the book down.

There are three parts to long-term memory. Keeping information stored away is actually the middle part. The first part is in fact related to our attention span. A lot of people who feel that they have memory problems may actually have attention problems. You can't remember something if you can't pay attention long enough to store it away.

In a similar vein, what good is reading something if you can't retain the information? In this sense, if you have to slow down to find a speed where you can remember everything, that's the fastest you can read. So it makes sense to work on both how fast you can take in information and how well you can retain it.

This is not the first time you will hear this recurring theme in this book, and it is far from the last: *Stop multitasking.*

If you need to pay attention to what you're reading in order to retain the information, then it makes sense that you are not paying attention to anything else. According to Clifford Nass of Stanford University, "The research is almost unanimous, which is very rare in social science, and it says that people who chronically multitask show an enormous range of deficits. They're basically terrible at all sorts of cognitive tasks, including multitasking" (Flatow, 2013). According to *Brain-Based Techniques for Retention of Information*, a study showed that "participants lost significant amounts of time as they switched between multiple tasks and lost even more time as the tasks became increasingly complex" (2019).

Retaining information as you read it is definitely a cognitive task, and even processing short texts can be a complex task. Just think about how often you have received a text that was a bit murky or required you to think about the intricacies of your schedule for the next few days before you could even start to form a reply. Now just imagine how difficult it is to read an organic chemistry text or Shakespeare!

It's true that there is such a thing as divided attention, or the ability to keep track of separate things. Functional magnetic resonance imaging (fMRI) scans of peoples' brains as well as monitoring signals based on the blood-oxygen levels in different areas of the brain showed that when doing two tasks at a time, there was no difference in brain activity from doing the tasks separately (Hahn et al., 2008). So, yes, you can learn to walk and chew gum at the same time, but you can't read a book and write a different one at the same time.

The important point is that we take learning and retaining information for granted, and not making that mistake is the real key to learning and reading effectively. Even having passive input like talk radio, TV, or social media can ruin your performance and result in having to reread a passage, or worse, skip over it without gaining anything from it.

One of the keys to retaining information is the universal truth, "use it or lose it." Some people say they don't learn things well by reading, and that is no doubt true, but it's also important to know whether the information has been fully processed. Retention involves doing something else with the information after it's been absorbed. Reading how to do something should be followed by putting the method into practice, working on problems, or explaining it to someone else (*Brain-Based Techniques*, 2019).

Reading for speed means making the input stage of reading efficient but also finding effective ways to process and internalize what you've read. While those seem to be conflicting processes if the goal is speed, reading and comprehending are not adversaries. You do need to coordinate them so that both can happen as quickly as possible.

Nobody taught you to think past the decoding part of reading when you learned to read. Focusing your attention on the problem of how to process the information is something that is probably beyond a first-grade student. Now it is part of learning speed reading and is something that will be greatly rewarding.

Summary

Reading is both a mental and physical activity that we learned when we were young and when our brains and bodies had not fully matured. It takes a set of habits to do a complex task because, cognitively, we can't do more than one task well at a time. You heard, and will again, that you must *stop multitasking*.

There are several layers of cognitive processing that happen when we read, and by having a better idea of what's going on, we can develop new habits and mental processes that allow us to take full advantage of our mature brains and bodies and optimize our reading.

You saw that attention and memory are related and that they are key to acquiring and retaining information. You also heard that repetition is part of the process, but it doesn't have to be oppressive.

The next chapter will talk about how we can make these changes in our habits. You'll see how habits work and how to form new ones, and after that, we can get into the specific techniques you can use to read more effectively.

Chapter 2:
Forming New Habits

Reading Is a Set of Habits

In order to read more effectively, you are going to do some training, and you're going to need to form some habits. Habits are things that we do automatically (*Habit Formation*, 2020). When you do a complex task, like riding a bicycle, you seem to be doing a lot of things simultaneously, but what you have really done is learned a set of habits.

Reading is a complex task. Even when you are reading slowly, there are a lot of things going on at the same time. You have to focus your eyes on the page, find the line you want, look at a letter, recognize its shape, see the letters around it, decode it, understand the word, remember the context of what you're reading, and on it goes.

If you had to concentrate and walk through the process step-by-step, it would be impossible. Again, think of riding a bike or hitting a golf ball. If we didn't have the ability to group ideas and learn to do things by habit, we would never be able to keep track of all the tiny variables in our heads at the same time, and we certainly couldn't pay attention to that many separate tasks. Habits are not multitasking, but they are an efficient way of programming some things to happen automatically (*Habit Formation*, 2020).

The habits you developed when you learned to read are limiting. For example, kids are told to "sound the words out" in order to understand them, but adult readers do not need to do this aloud, and if they did, it would take all day to get through a newspaper. So you are taught to read "in your head," but most people have an inner voice. This habit is called "subvocalization" and is an improvement over reading aloud, but it is a limiting factor in how fast we read (Halton, 2019).

It's not helpful to call these "bad" habits or to say that you have habits you need to "break." This suggests that there's a problem, a deficit, something to be repaired. It also carries the negative connotations of addictive behaviors, like smoking or gambling habits. They did serve a purpose, but that job is done, so the habits are not needed anymore.

It's much more accurate and positive to think that you are going to learn *new* habits. You are going to develop habits that are oriented toward *performance*, not just reading competence. It's not enough to read accurately, which you have already learned to do; now it's time to train for speed.

A good comparison, bringing back the image of bicycles, is that when you were a kid, you used training wheels to ride a bike. That was fine for just playing around, but now you want to move into competitive cycling. Nobody in the Tour de France uses training wheels. You will need to learn the habits that will keep you in the race.

Routine Becomes Reflex

Probably the most powerful way to build a habit is to make an action into a routine. A routine is a repeated activity done on a *regular* basis. Regular here means that it repeats steadily: every day, every week, every hour, or whatever it may be. The amount of time is not the important thing; the important thing is that it happens periodically and without fail.

A routine might be that you take a walk after dinner every day, rain or shine. If you were to keep this up for 20 years, it would probably feel a little disturbing if you were not able to take your walk. People get used to routines and start to expect them. This is the first sign that a routine is starting to become a reflex.

A reflex is also something you do regularly, but instead of doing the thing because the clock or calendar says it's time to, you do it because it is your innate reaction to some outside stimulus. When the phone rings, you want to answer it. As a little psychological experiment, you might notice how much it bothers people when you *don't* answer a phone. Even if you say, "It's alright, I'll let it go to voicemail," people are still edgy until the ringing stops.

This is an example of reflexive behavior, or conditioned response. You are probably aware of the story of Pavlov and his dogs. It was known that the dogs would salivate when given food, but by putting a metronome on when the dogs were fed, they eventually learned to salivate for only the sound of the metronome (Mcleod, 2018). When the phone rings, we are conditioned to respond to it.

What you have to learn to stay focused is a little different—you have to train yourself that when you are reading, the response to an outside stimulus is to keep reading rather than give in. You can think of it as having to *ignore* the outside stimulus, or you can think of it as being spurred on to read *more*. Like the child who reads by flashlight under their covers after bedtime, when told to stop and go to sleep, their response is to just read faster!

By making an activity routine, repetition starts to make it reflexive. Not only is this valuable in paying attention and maintaining self-discipline, but it is a way to change your reading habits. The good news is the process works for both physical habits that slow you down and also for mental habits that improve processing and retention.

Forming New Habits Is Better and Easier

It is more positive and effective to think about forming new habits than it is to try and break "bad" habits. We all know people who struggle and put themselves through a lot of stress because they feel like they are failing to change a bad habit, like smoking. Don't think of the process of learning speed reading as one that is trying to correct a mistake, think of it as learning a new way to do something.

It's also easier to train yourself to *do* something than it is to train yourself to *stop* doing something. Here is a detailed description of how forming new habits works so you can understand what is going on and how to be effective when you want to turn the techniques of speed reading described later in this book into habits. This is, at least in part, the training program you will be starting.

Set a Goal

If you haven't defined what you're trying to achieve, it's difficult to know when you have done it. You have to be specific, though. If your goal is only "I want to read faster," then that's either too vague—how fast is fast enough?—or too easy. You need to be clear and say, "I want to increase my reading speed by 10 words per minute every day," or, "I will extend my reading practice by five minutes every two days." When you set a goal, you should be using numbers in some way so that you can measure your progress quantitatively.

Make a Plan

After you set a goal, you need a detailed plan. You should be breaking tasks into small pieces so that you don't feel like you are sitting down to eat a moose—something you can't do in one sitting. This will keep you on track to your ultimate goal, but you will also be able to concentrate on the piece in front of you. An occasional glance at the summit is nice to see your progress, but when you're climbing Mount Everest, you spend a lot more time looking at your next step.

When you break your goal up into steps, you should be specific about exactly what you will do and when you will do it. Even better than saying "I will practice speed reading every day" is to say something like "I will train for reading 10 minutes every day before breakfast and 10 minutes after lunch." If you lock it into your schedule, it's not just something that you are hoping to get done, life permitting, maybe, if it doesn't rain. You are establishing that it is important enough to have a place in your schedule and that other things must take a back seat for those particular minutes (Milkman, 2021).

The other point here is to make your goals based on a cue, like finishing lunch, rather than just a time. This way, you can use the same technique to work on habits outside of scheduling, and you will have provided a way that will lead naturally to forming a reflex, not just a routine.

Repeat Regularly

You've heard it before: Repetition is the key. A lot of people in North America have gotten the idea that repetition is a waste of time and a bad way to learn things, but that completely ignores the fact that it is *exactly* how we really do learn certain things. According to The CPD Certification Service, "When stimuli are learned by repetition, they are remembered better and retained for a longer time [...] optimizing performance of the skill" (2022).

But repetition can be off-putting if it is mindless or mechanical. If you find that you dread having to train or practice, you will start to avoid it. The solution is to find a way to make it fun or enjoyable.

If you are a competitive person, you might try and beat your personal best. If you are more social, maybe you can do a "buddy system" and find a partner to train with. If you are a book lover, then you can use whatever your current favorite novel is as the subject material—up to a point. (We'll discuss what kind of material you should use for practice later.)

You can offer yourself treats if you make it through 15 minutes of solid concentration, but choose wisely. If you reward yourself with a donut every 15 minutes, you'll end up spoiling your supper, gaining weight, and raising your cholesterol! Even so, it is important to emphasize the desirable points of what you're doing. As the saying goes, "If you enjoy what you're doing, it's not work."

Don't Be Too Rigid

If you were training as a cyclist or runner and had to set a personal best every time you trained, you would inevitably fail. If you set the goal that you were going to win every race or you would quit the sport, everyone in their right mind would say that's ridiculous.

Some days are better than others, and the day you stop trying to improve is the day you guarantee that you won't improve any more. When you're creating a habit, regular practice is key, but that doesn't mean it's the end of the world if you get stuck at work or have a personal crisis that forces you to skip practice that day.

Patterns are what is most important. If you have established a pattern of training every day, but you miss one occasionally, that's fine. If you have good intentions to practice every day but *actually practice* one day out of 10, then the pattern isn't a good one. Try and keep your average up, but don't beat yourself up if you aren't perfect.

Similarly, if you make a lot of progress for two weeks and then seem to hit a plateau, don't get upset or think that you've reached the end of the road. Sometimes that happens while your brain is building up new pathways. Knowing when to take a day off to let things sink in is tricky but sometimes necessary.

Tell Your Friends

Another way to make habits become ingrained is to tell others. If your friends know that you practice reading at a certain time, it makes it more "real" to you, and it might catch on. It's a great help to be part of a community that shares an interest, and a little friendly competition to see who can make the biggest increase in a week, for example, also makes the whole thing more fun.

How Long Does It Take?

Developing new habits isn't an overnight process. If repetition is the key, then how many times do you have to repeat something before it becomes a conditioned response? There's no magic number of repetitions or number of days. A commonly held but incorrect belief is that if you do something for 21 days, it will become a habit (King, 2020).

A big factor is how happy you are when you perform the new behavior. Think of a kid at a carnival. They might be apprehensive about getting on a roller coaster at first, but after the ride, some kids are so exhilarated that they pester their parents relentlessly, "Let's do that again!" The trick to building a new habit is to generate that kind of reaction to a stimulus and repeat it. (Of course, the story is exaggerated—you shouldn't need to be that overstimulated to make progress!)

But the moral of the story is that it's not something that you should judge by the amount of time that has passed. If you see a list of dates where you have written down how many words per minute you read, pay more attention to your speed and how it's increasing than to the number of days or hours you spent getting there. Don't give the date any thought at all. There's no deadline to meet. Improvement is improvement.

How to Make New Habits Stick

In a sense, you already know how to make new habits stick—repeat something until it becomes second nature. Set a goal and make a plan. The goal might be to read 500 words per minute, about twice the average reading speed (David, 2012). If you already read 250 words per minute, you might need to break that up into smaller sub-goals.

So, more specifically, you might set a weekly goal of increasing your speed by 50 words per minute per week. That would mean your sub-goal could be accomplished by increasing by 10 words per minute per day, but it would also leave you a little safety margin. So then you might also say that you are going to read for 20 minutes in the morning and 20 minutes after lunch.

If each of those sessions were timed, you would want to read 200 more words each session. This is an ambitious goal, but not an impossible one. The nice thing about the safety margin is that it will allow you to have a bad day, or one where the phone won't stop ringing or you need to deal with whatever may come up.

Another way to plan things in order to make things stick is to look at habits in terms of the habit cycle, as explained by James Clear (2018). In this analysis, there are four stages of a habit:

1. Cue

2. Craving

3. Response

4. Reward

Simple cues are basic needs like hunger, but we can have other cues, like wanting praise or to feel secure when we look at our checkbook. The cue we want to develop here is a desire to read quickly, so in this case, seeing a book or reading material might be a cue for us to want to know how quickly we can read it.

The step of craving is when the cue makes us itchy to do something. We see a picture of a beautiful meal, and we want to stop working and go to lunch. The point that Clear makes is that you want to feel the change that happens when you satisfy the craving (2018). It's not about the dish you see; it's about feeling full instead of hungry. So with reading, it's more abstract. Rather than wanting to *have* a book, you want to feel the difference between not knowing what it contains and having learned what it contains.

That brings you to the response, or what you do in response to the craving. Do you put up with it, or do you address it? The part you want to pay great attention to when speed reading is *how* you address it. Obviously, if the craving is to read the book or other material, the response is to read it, but we want to make a much more detailed response of reading efficiently. The techniques for speed reading that follow are sub-habits that crop up during the process of reading, but the same habit loop exists on a smaller scale.

The final step, the reward, is the payoff. This is where you get a good feeling, a sense of pride, and it makes you want to go on the roller coaster again. Everything points at the reward—the cue stage is where you first think about the reward, the craving is when your desire for the reward blooms, and the response is when you take steps to claim the reward. In the case of speed reading, the reward is learning the information, finishing the task, setting a new speed record, having more free time— there are quite a few rewards.

If you get rewarded, you want to keep doing the things that gave you that reward, and this is why the habit loop makes for new habits that stick. Practicing regularly so that you get the reward regularly is necessary to really make these habits permanent, and best of all, it is a positive feedback cycle. The more you do it, the more you want to do it, and the easier it gets, and the faster your progress.

Summary

This chapter showed you how habits are simply ways we perform tasks as a response to different stimuli and that they are part of how we read. If we want to read faster, we have to change our habits. You have seen that repetition is important, that doing things regularly can turn routines into habits, and that in order to do this consciously, you need to make a detailed plan.

There is no set time limit for how quickly new habits become established, but with regular practice and frequent, satisfying rewards, they will take root quicker and more effectively. Understanding the loop of habitual behavior makes it easy to form the detailed plan you need to be successful.

In the next chapter, we will look at some of the physical techniques of reading. The idea is that you will be able to take what you know about forming habits and apply that knowledge in order to make the physical component of your reading more efficient and graceful.

Chapter 3:
Physical Techniques

Small Improvements Multiply Quickly

If someone asked you to name three physical activities, you'd probably say things like running, working on an oil well, or weight lifting. It would be really easy to scoff and argue that reading isn't a physical activity at all. In fact, if you say that someone is "bookish," the image that comes to mind is someone who is pale and slight in build.

It's true that reading doesn't require great physical strength, but in terms of the sheer number of times you move muscles, reading shifts to a much higher rank. This counts the movements of the arms and hands turning pages and the movements of the muscles that aim and adjust the focus of the eyes. There are six muscles attached to each eye, and they are in constant use when you read (Red Apple Dyslexia Association, 2021).

So while it is true that you are making small motions, more like using fine motor skills, you make up for that in volume when you're reading. If, for example, you move your eyes five times to read a line, and there are typically 40 lines on a printed page, that's 200 movements, plus another 40 to go to the beginning of the next line, for a total of at least 240 movements per page. If you are reading a 200-page book, that's 48,000 eye movements—and that's assuming you didn't have to go back to reread anything! Do you still think that reading isn't a physical activity?

No, reading doesn't make you an athlete, but it does require that you make many, many motions. If you can make even a 1% increase in the efficiency of your reading motions, the benefit would be multiplied by 48,000 in our example. Even a small difference will have a big effect.

Being Physically Efficient

In terms of physical movements, we're going to separate eye *movement* from visual adjustments and what's called fixation. This section will be concerned with economy of motion in order to avoid repeating things unnecessarily. The next chapter is where you will learn about techniques that have more to do with your eyesight. Some thoughts on turning pages efficiently are also coming up.

Don't Backtrack

The worst possible way to do a task quickly is by doing it twice. If you have to reread a passage, your speed is effectively cut in half. That's like the difference between the speed of driving on the highway compared to the speed of driving down a city street. Perhaps a more stark comparison would be having to drive twice as far to go from your house to work every day. This is a difference you would give serious thought to if you were choosing where to live or work.

There are two ways people can end up rereading. The first is known as "regression," which is when you go back on purpose, often because you realize you haven't understood a passage (Gaid, 2020).

If you go back to enjoy the beauty of a particularly well-written passage, that's fine—not all reading needs to be speed reading. Making a conscious choice to go back over material is fine and sometimes necessary. If you're rereading for other reasons, then you probably want to eliminate those reasons, including regression.

Most of the ways to deal with regression are mental things. You will want to improve your concentration and eliminate distractions so that you can have the best chance of understanding what you read the first time. Specific ways to do this will be covered in more detail in Chapter 5.

The second way you end up rereading is called "backtracking," or "back-skipping" (Gaid, 2020). This happens when your eyes move to another position on the page, which can happen if you blink or see movement in your field of vision, and sometimes even just a little twitch of your eye muscles can cause it. (It's perfectly normal.) The result is that you start reading from the point your eye lands on, and you might end up rereading something you don't need to.

Trackers & Pacers

There is a very simple tool that has real value known as a "tracker." A tracker is an object that is used to keep your eyes on track. Some people use their fingers, some people use a pen, others use a card, and if you get very fancy, you might even use a sheet with a window cut in it.

This is a little like when people put blinders on a horse to prevent it from being distracted by things going on around it. This method was common in order to keep the horse from getting distracted or spooked in busy cities where there was a lot of commotion and traffic.

Using your finger to read helps your eye to focus on the text you are reading. It draws your eye to the word that you're on and keeps it from wandering, which results in backtracking. While you don't have to use them all the time, anytime you need a little boost in concentration and focus, a tracker offers a little mental assistance by making the physical eye work a little easier (Beale & Mullan, 2008).

There is more to using a finger as a tracer than just putting it under the word you're reading. To begin with, this simply isn't the most efficient method. The other drawback is that it is the most likely to make you feel a little self-conscious.

If you see someone reading intently, following each word with their finger, your first impression might be that they are having difficulty. That isn't necessarily the case at all. Even if it were, you shouldn't worry about what anyone else thinks about how you read. You do what you need to do to get the job done. As the old folk saying goes, "What other people think of you is none of your business!"

That said, it's more effective to drag your finger down the page as you read rather than move along each line. You have a few choices for where to place your finger when using just one—the left side, middle, or right side of the column of text. Putting your finger on the left side of the page gives your eyes a target to hit when they reach the end of the line and return to the beginning of the next.

By moving your finger a little faster than you are currently reading, you can think of it as a goal to finish the line before your finger has reached the next line so that they meet at the same time. This is known as "pacing." You can use your tracker to not only keep track of your position but also to set the pace of your reading.

You can do the same thing with your finger on the right side of the column instead. Again, you can use your finger as a target, only this time you read toward it. You can also put your finger in the middle of a column of text. This is very effective when reading narrow columns of text, but more on that in Chapter 4.

There are variations of this technique: using more than one finger at a time, putting one finger at each end of the line of text, and so forth. There are other patterns you can use, too, such as the "Z" pattern, where you scan across the first line, and then return to the left margin a few lines lower than where you started (Beale & Mullan, 2008). The pattern is repeated as you move down the page.

Using a card or piece of paper can keep a whole line in focus, but there's a very simple way to do this that makes regression and backtracking impossible: Put the paper at the *top* of the line that you want to read. If you put a card or paper under the line you are reading, you have a great view of everything that you have already read and no way to read ahead, but if you put the paper *above* the line you are reading, it is impossible to even see what you have already read.

Another way to use a card is to find one that is wide enough to cover the whole line with a bit of extra space that extends beyond the edges of the text. Cut a window or slit in it that will allow you to read one or two lines of text. This is very helpful for keeping you focused. Making the window more than one line tall allows you to keep reading as you get to the end of the second line because you will also need to be moving the card down the page.

When you use a card in this way, it is sometimes called a "pacer" as opposed to a "tracker." A pacer is a tracker that is used to set the pace of your tracking, but there isn't any need to get too fussy about the terms. The function is to keep your eyes from backtracking, prevent rereading, and help you concentrate on the material. Both fingers and cards can be used to set the pace.

Page Turning

The idea with turning pages is to keep your arm and hand out of your field of vision. You can choose to reach around the top of the page with your left hand, or you can use your right hand at the bottom of the page. Whichever hand you are not using to turn pages is the one that will be left to do any tracking or pacing.

When you turn the pages, you want to do it crisply and quickly, but also smoothly. Remember that your goal is to keep your eyes busy reading, not skipping around or trying to find your place. Using cards makes page turning more awkward, but that doesn't mean that they aren't useful for training. There is a difference between practice and actual reading, but that will be covered more fully in Chapter 7.

If it seems like you won't be able to use these techniques while in your favorite chair for reading, then you are perceptive. You want to sit at a desk or table so that you can spread out, sit properly, and have room to work. Lying on a couch reading sounds like a relaxing way to spend your time, but it is not conducive to the level of focus you need, at least not until you are in very good form. There will be more information on arranging your environment in Chapter 7 as well.

Summary

You have seen that, physically, there are some actions people make that slow down their reading. Because these are often at least partially involuntary, it helps to have some physical aids that keep your eyes on track and that you can use to set and maintain a pace. Whether you use your fingers or paper cards, you will avoid backtracking, and it will help you focus your attention and reduce rereading.

While the physical motions of the eyes are important, in the next chapter, you will learn some of the things we do with our eyes in terms of vision. You will then see how to use that to gain a further speed advantage and take care of your eyes.

Chapter 4:
Visual Techniques

Healthy Eyes

As I mentioned in Chapter 1, it is assumed that your vision falls within normal parameters. That means it's considered "correctable" with glasses or contact lenses to give you 20/20 vision. But you don't actually have to have 20/20 vision. Some people who are nearsighted may read without glasses at all, and farsighted people might want reading glasses in order to read.

In fact, it's important to get your vision checked regularly, even if you don't wear glasses (Taylor, 2022). This helps monitor for health issues that can develop as you age, like cataracts and glaucoma, but it's also important for ensuring your eyes are not making reading difficult in ways you might not catch at first. This can show up in hidden ways, like realizing that you don't read as much as you used to "for some reason."

If you have headaches when you read, or if you find that you get tired easily when reading, it's a very good idea to see your eye doctor. If it seems like everything you read is boring or hard to "get into," it might be that you are suffering from some visual discomfort. While it might not be "pain," per se, it's still the visual equivalent of having a stone in your shoe, and it's a lot easier to walk if you address the issue.

If you do have issues with your eyesight, such as poor peripheral vision or more serious issues like macular degeneration, it does not mean you cannot learn to read faster. It might mean that some of the techniques are not going to be as effective for you or that you will want to modify them. But many of the techniques, such as building your vocabulary and doing timed readings, are going to work to some degree.

If you don't have perfect vision, it could mean that your maximum speed is going to be a little lower than somebody else's, but the only competition that matters is trying to beat yourself. It is important to remember that what you really want to see is a percentage improvement over your past performance rather than achieving a fixed number of words per minute.

Eye Strain

You have probably heard the term "eye strain" and seen products that offer relief. Generally, eye strain can be anything from a bothersome annoyance to something that teaches you to avoid doing certain tasks in the worst case. It is rarely serious but should be taken seriously in case it is actually a sign of a true condition.

Eye strain occurs any time you use your eyes intensely, and the less you move your eyes around, the more likely you are to get it. Using computer screens or driving long distances are activities where it can occur, and certainly reading for long periods of time is another (Mayo Clinic, 2022a).

The symptoms of eye strain can include headaches and migraines, pain in the neck and shoulders, or vision that gets blurry (Taylor, 2022). They can also include burning or itchy eyes, being unusually sensitive to light, feeling like your eyes won't stay open, or even just having difficulty concentrating (Mayo Clinic, 2022a). Of course, all of these can be symptoms of other problems, so if resting your eyes doesn't bring relief, check with your eye-care professional or doctor.

If you find that you have strained your eyes, resting them is the way to fix things. It's easy to see how that will slow you down if you are trying to read quickly. In fact, the best way you can prevent eye strain is by resting your eyes periodically *before* it starts to be a problem.

Try following the 20-20-20 rule, which says that after doing a task for 20 minutes, you should look at something at least 20 feet away for a good 20 seconds (Taylor, 2022). This gives the muscles in the eyes a chance to relax and stretch, so to speak. You rest the scanning muscles that move the eyes, and you change the focus of the eyes by making them focus on something at a different distance.

Another way you can reduce your risk of eye strain is by making sure you have enough light. The ambient light in a room may not be enough for an intense, visual task like reading. If you have light coming from behind or above you, glare becomes a concern, but a shaded desk lamp or reading lamp that keeps the direct light out of your eyes is a good choice (Mayo Clinic, 2022b). You might need to close the curtains if there is a lot of bright sunlight.

If you're reading on a screen, whether a computer, tablet, or phone, you should have brighter light in the room than the device is producing. If the screen is the brightest thing in your field of vision, you will have eye strain from the glare conditions (Taylor, 2022). Turn the brightness down as far as you can while still being able to read comfortably.

You should also adjust the contrast, which is the difference between light and dark, turning it down as well. Putting your monitor in a window is generally a bad idea, even if it is tempting to enjoy the view, as it makes for a lot of contrast when it is bright out—your pupils will try to contract, making it hard to read. A stark-white wall behind your monitor can also cause trouble, but if painting a soft color is not an option, you can consider putting a cloth or piece of paper up with blue tack or double-sided tape.

Your general health affects your eyes and vice versa. If you are tired and hungry, your eyes are also tired (and hungry). Make sure you are sleeping regularly and that you're getting enough sleep. This will also pay off in maximizing your ability to concentrate.

Likewise, if you are plodding away, struggling to read in conditions that strain your eyes, then eye strain can lead to the symptoms mentioned earlier, including headaches, migraine headaches, muscle aches, and more. If your sleep is disrupted, you can get into a really vicious circle. If your eyes start to tire, it tires you, and that makes reading harder, which tires your eyes. But if you can stay out of trouble and build your stamina, you will not just read better, you may begin to feel better generally.

Move Your Eyes Less

You have already seen how many movements the eyes make when you read. Thousands and thousands. There are two parts to this: When your eyes stop on a word to decode it, it is called "fixating," and the motion your eyes make when they move on to the next word is known as "saccading" (Beale & Mullan, 2008). It's not actually the motions that are the problem. In a sense, the eyes only move when they have to gather more visual information.

If you had to look at each letter, like kindergarteners have to, the number of fixations you would be making in a line of text would be the same as the number of letters. When you get better at reading, you only need to look at a whole word, so you have fewer fixations and can therefore read faster. To read even faster, you want to look at groups of words or even whole lines. The number of letters or words that you can see at one time is known as the "eye span," or the number of words the eye spans, or covers, at one time (Beale & Mullan, 2008).

Eye span is one of the specific things that stop developing after the first few grades of school. It is also one of the most important things in improving your reading speed. By moving to a wider eye span, you can take in more words at a time, reducing the number of fixations you have to make per line. So, in effect, by working on this one trait, you get twice the benefit.

Here is an example of what this would look like. A person who moves their eyes to fixate on each word would read thus:

Reading bigger groups returns a big increase in efficiency and speed.

That is 11 words. If each fixation required 250 milliseconds, that would take 2.75 seconds to read. A little better would be:

Reading bigger groups returns a big increase in efficiency and speed.

That is only four groups, yet each takes roughly the same 250 milliseconds to process. Therefore, this line would take about 1 second to read. That is nearly three times as fast! With a little more practice, you could manage to do the following:

Reading bigger groups returns a big increase in efficiency and speed.

Reading these two groups would take only about half a second. And finally, reading the whole line at once would take about a quarter of a second, or 250 milliseconds:

Reading bigger groups returns a big increase in efficiency and speed.

Even if it took a little longer to process the whole line, say 275 milliseconds, the ratio between 2.75 seconds, or 2,750 milliseconds, and our faster speed is 10 more. No, not every line is going to show this much improvement. Lines with fewer long words don't have as many spaces to eliminate. But if you could increase your speed by even a factor of five, it would be a big improvement!

Peripheral Vision

The question that is begging to be asked is, "How do you expand your eye span to read bigger groups of words?" The answer is that you will practice using your peripheral vision more and not only rely on your central vision. According to Yu et al., the biggest reason people seek help from low-vision clinics is difficulty with reading (2018). There have been studies done with the goal of training people to use their peripheral vision to overcome reading difficulties.

The evidence showed that people who increased their eye span from 0.7 to 1.9 letters more than it was before training were able to read between 41–66% faster (Yu et al., 2018). This confirms the benefits shown in the previous example of reducing the number of fixations you make while reading a line of text.

However, without training, peripheral vision has been shown to have a reduced eye span compared to central vision (Legge et al., 2001). While the training isn't difficult, it is necessary to build the habits discussed in Chapter 2 that will expand the eye span in your peripheral vision. This leads to better, faster, and more accurate letter recognition and a higher overall reading speed. Again, it is the *improvement*, not the final number, that is the most important thing.

When you want to use your peripheral vision, the first thing you should do is practice softening your gaze. Look at a page of text and pick one letter near the center. Focus on this letter only, concentrating on its shape. Now let your eyes relax and become aware of the whole page— you won't be able to see the first letter as clearly, but you will become aware of the full line in which it sits, and then the whole page. Try and make your eyes act like they do when you're just staring into space as if you aren't really looking at the page.

This is a good exercise for the muscles in your eyes, but it's also a good way to rest your eyes if you start feeling fatigued. If you find yourself in a small room, this can take the place of finding something 20 feet away if you want to use the 20-20-20 rule.

Narrow Columns

It would certainly seem that reading narrow columns of text would be a lot faster. This is true and was very well-known by typesetters, printers, and journalists almost 200 years ago. Did you ever wonder why newspapers and magazines are printed in narrow columns? Precisely because it is easier and faster to read. The reader's eye doesn't have to move as far from the end of the line to the beginning, and it doesn't have to make as many fixations to get from one end of a line to another.

Wide columns are harder, or at least slower, to read. Advertising will often try to use the full width of a page for the text, partly because it might look nice, but also because it makes you linger over the page that much longer. If you need to generate documents that can be read quickly, then remember that there is a big advantage for the reader when you use three columns per page instead of the full width.

Using a card to track and pace down a column is still helpful to prevent backtracking. Skipping out of the column that you are reading into other columns isn't generally a concern. The space between columns is usually enough of a cue that your eyes know to stop there. If you did find your eye wandering into another column, you could always cover those columns with a sheet of paper.

You could also make a window paper with a hole of only one to two lines of print tall and just as wide as a column. The window should be cut out of the exact center of the page. You don't need to cover all the text on the page that you aren't reading, you only need to make a clear boundary between what you're reading and any text that might be distracting.

Margins

If the idea of narrow columns is to reduce the size of a line to something that can be read in one fixation, it removes the need to use peripheral vision, but if a book is printed with wide lines of text, you either have to move your eyes or use your peripheral vision. To help you make that transition, you can use "virtual margins," or cue your eyes in another way that will help you read long lines.

The first way to do it would be to use the index fingers of both hands at the same time like trackers. Do not put them at the ends of the lines, but instead put them about one to two words in from the edges (Gaid, 2020). This gives your eye a cue to make a fixation, and it is also fairly natural to use the center of the text as a fixation (unless the page is very wide— but shame on the book designer if it is!).

This helps you practice reading the page making only three fixations per line, and you can try softening your gaze and using your peripheral vision. After a while, you can move your fingers so they divide the lines into thirds. Now see if you can move your eyes just twice, one fixation at each finger. If you find that you are still having trouble with backtracking, instead of using your fingers, you can draw two lines or dots on a piece of paper and use it in the same places you would put your fingers. Adapt this to any sort of tracker you like.

Another idea is to get some acetate sheets at an office supply store or plastic page protectors and draw the guidelines on there. Be sure to use a fine marker that won't obscure too much of the text while you're reading it. This way you can put the guidelines over the pages and just move the overlay, and it saves you from drawing lines in your reading material.

You *could* draw lines if the book belongs to you, but besides defacing things that might not belong to you, the problem is that you may improve your peripheral vision to the point where only one line down the center is sufficient. If you are able to read a line with only one fixation, then having cues to make more fixations could actually slow you down later.

Summary

Taking care of your eyes is important, and that includes not straining them by working too hard without a break. You have learned that it's important to have good lighting conditions, and you know how to adjust your screens so that glare and strain are kept to a minimum. Moving your eyes less, thus making fewer "fixations" on a line of text, and improving your use of peripheral vision are going to be useful tools to put in your toolbox for improving your reading speed. You also know that narrower columns of text are faster to read and that simulating them can help you use your peripheral vision more.

In the next chapter, we'll cover techniques that will improve what goes on inside your head after your eyes have processed the text. This will let you do a little spring cleaning and keep the habits that are helpful and put the things that hinder you into the back of the closet or send them to the dump.

Chapter 5:
Mental Techniques

Eliminate Subvocalizing

If you read aloud to yourself, you are certainly not reading as quickly as someone who doesn't. It is a technique that does have its uses, such as when learning a new language or when it's absolutely critical to understand something. If reading aloud is something you do habitually, then, as the first step in reading faster, you should challenge yourself to stop and read silently.

Most likely you already read "in your head," but when you do so, you hear an inner voice saying the words. This is known as "subvocalizing," or some people call it "mental whispering" (Beale & Mullan, 2008). Once again, it limits the speed at which you are reading, because you have a tendency to adjust to a good tempo for listening. In fact, we can read much faster than we can understand words aurally.

Since your ears are not necessary for reading, it turns out that subvocalization is not really necessary for reading. How can you change this habit and build a new one? The first step is to notice it (Troester, 2023). You can then start to build the loop of habit forming discussed in Chapter 2.

If the cue is to read something, the craving should be considered to be reading it without subvocalizing. The response would be to use a technique or attempt to read it without subvocalizing, and the reward would be the feeling of satisfaction you get from succeeding. If you need to motivate yourself more directly, you could give yourself a treat or piece of candy when you are successful, but the danger there is overeating or developing other habits as a result.

It might be a little bit difficult to tell whether you have stopped subvocalizing or not. It is something already very internal, so you might time yourself reading a page and set goals from there. Keep a sheet of paper or a note in your phone showing how often you hit your goal. For example, you could take a small book and time how long it takes to read a page, then say that you want to read the next page five seconds faster.

We will discuss in greater detail in Chapter 9 how to do timed readings and measure your reading speed. At this stage, you just need to understand that you can change one variable at a time or work on one particular aspect of reading and measure your progress by the result you see in your reading speed. If you get faster, then it must be that you have made improvement in subvocalization, in this case.

There are several particular techniques you can use to tell your inner voice to shut up! A good approach is to tie it up doing something else. While you read, try counting, like marking beats in music. "One, two, three, four, one, two, three, four," or you might prefer "one, two, three, one, two, three" (Troester, 2023). You will see later that this can be done in conjunction with a metronome as well.

Repeating a simple syllable, such as "la la la la" also works. Don't get too fancy—trying to say the alphabet while you are reading is going to get confusing. The point isn't to learn to pat your head and rub your stomach at the same time; the point is just to distract your brain enough that you can quiet the inner voice.

Grouping

Reading groups of words rather than single words is something you can benefit from visually as well as mentally. Not only does it allow you to make fewer fixations, but it also helps to quiet the inner voice. All the techniques for improving your peripheral vision will be useful here. Soften your gaze, draw margins, and perhaps even hold the book a bit further back so that you can take in more text at a time (Troester, 2023).

For practice, you can try working with two window cards. One should have the normal window exposing a line of text, and you can make another to go over it that allows you to see, for example, a third of the line at a time. Another way to practice reading groups is by using the computer. Some more examples will be given in Chapter 9.

Another way to practice grouping is to pay attention to common phrases. There are blocks of words that come all at once, expressions and phrases that are a regular part of ordinary speech. For instance, "lady of the house," "skinny as a beanpole," or even just ordinary phrases such as "thank you," "please call me," or "at your earliest convenience" are all groups of words that occur together. If you can recognize them as a single phrase, it saves a lot of time decoding and processing each word.

If it feels like this is impossible, just remember that languages like Chinese and Japanese have complex characters that can represent a very complex idea that requires several words to say. It's definitely not impossible. There are literally billions of people in Asia who think this way. But it *is* foreign to English speakers. The trick is to get your brain and eye to recognize "at your earliest convenience," or any phrase you like, as *one* so-called character.

It's not enough to just tell you to find some common phrases and read them as one character. You should compile a list. Websites and books that teach people English are good sources for common phrases, but you will want to modify them based on what seems to be more common in your own life and correspondence. One website in particular you could start with is www.englishspeak.com/en/english-phrases.

In a way, this is the beginning of trying to stack the deck in your favor, which is a powerful technique for increasing your reading speed. If you already know what a group of words says, you don't have to spend nearly as long reading it. This is how grouping works, and you'll hear more about this idea in Chapter 6 and again in Chapter 9.

Focus

If you are not focused, you are not reading as fast as you possibly could. Distractions and interruptions can come from external sources, or they can be internal. External distractions are easy to spot, and they also let us shift the blame for not continuing. "I couldn't read because X was happening."

If you have children, the odds are good that picking up a book is a magnet for them to come ask for things. And this isn't limited to kids. Husbands, wives, coworkers, pets—it seems that all of them can get in the way of reading. Clearly they count as external distractions, as do noises, flickering lights, smells, and probably more things than you can think of.

You don't have to be at the mercy of external distractions. Most of the time you can take steps to abate them, and it isn't just a case of having superpowers or being able to tune things out by sheer force of will. Sure, with practice you might be able to do this, but you should not feel bad if it isn't easy.

Some people can lose themselves in their headphones and a book on a noisy, crowded bus or subway, but other people just aren't able to make that work for them. Other people can't stand the thought of being trapped alone in a silent room and need a certain amount of noise or stimulation to stay on task. The point is to understand the steps that *you* need to take so that you can focus without interruption.

Additionally, there are internal distractions. Feeling hungry or tired or finding that your thoughts wander to what's going to happen at a meeting later in the week are all examples of internal distractions. You will want to recognize when you are having internal distractions so that you can redirect your attention and energy to the task you want to accomplish.

There are a couple of broad categories of techniques for staying focused and on task.

Reducing Distractions

Our first instinct is to hide or find a quiet space when we are faced with too many distractions. Go with that—it's the right thing to do. You should be in a space where you won't be disturbed. An office is better than the family activity of the living room. A library is good. Coffeehouses can be good for some people because even though there is sometimes a crowd, they are not likely to bother you (Chia, 2021).

Another way to have a little space is to set boundaries regarding time. If you treat reading like a meeting and tell your family or coworkers that you are not available, then it helps send the message that reading is important, and it also reinforces that idea in your own mind.

Put your phone away out of reach, and if you're reading on a computer, close your social media and email apps. Not having distractions close at hand makes them far less tempting. It's very easy to switch to a different window "just for a second" or to take a "quick peek" at your texts, but it's really not worth the price you pay in terms of concentration.

There is something else that has been mentioned repeatedly that is a great source of distraction on so many levels: the dreaded *multitasking*. Don't do it. Another way to think of it is that instead of other people interrupting you, multitasking is you interrupting yourself!

Make sure that you have taken care of your physical needs. If you're hungry, thirsty, or have to use the bathroom, you will find it hard to concentrate. Think of reading like taking a car trip—if you keep stopping, a two-hour trip can take all afternoon. And in this case, make sure you go to the bathroom before you start reading!

Increasing Devotion

Besides decreasing the amount of distraction that is going on, you should try and increase your devotion to reading. If "devotion" seems like an odd word to use, it's worthwhile to think about what it means. Besides the religious sense of the word, devotion is "the act of dedicating something to a cause, enterprise, or activity: the act of devoting," or "the fact or state of being ardently dedicated and loyal" (Merriam-Webster, n.d.). So it's not enough to simply play defense against the external distractions that can steal your attention, you also have to play offense and devote yourself to the task of reading.

Some of the ways to be more devoted overlap with reducing distractions. Again, setting reading apart, even making it into a bit of a ritual, sets the stage for you to focus. Making sure that you are in a space that is open and not cluttered helps to make the book or page the most interesting thing around you. You don't have to be in a Japanese temple, but you don't want to be surrounded by too many papers, which remind you of the things you are *not* doing right now.

Being clear that you are not multitasking, you are *reading*, is a much bigger deal than it sounds at first. You might find it helpful to write down your goal for the day. If you write down your goal the night before, you will wake up thinking of that goal as a major part of your day (Chia, 2021). If you are training to read, you might have a goal of doubling your result on a timed reading. If you are actually reading, you might have a goal of so many words or pages within a given time limit. Waking up and knowing that's what you want to accomplish gives you stronger motivation when you are actually doing it.

Learning to "live in the moment" is also a skill to practice. When you sit to read, don't think about what you're going to do afterward. You cannot view reading as an obstacle between now and the next thing you want to do. You must say to yourself, "I am reading now," and make it what you want to be doing right now. The other thing will still be a thing you want to do, but it will have to wait until later.

Likewise, you don't want to run instant replays of whatever just happened before your reading, or two days ago. All that is important when you're reading is reading. It sounds simple, but you may not realize how often our mind is doing something other than we think it is or want it to be doing.

If you want to do some exercises that will help you build stamina with your attention span, much the same way athletes do strength training, you can practice mindfulness or meditate. The benefit is that these activities make you aware of what you are thinking about. By meditating, which involves clearing the mind, you learn to control when extraneous thoughts distract you from a task. Mindfulness exercises also help to keep you aware of what you're thinking and doing, so being distracted becomes a conscious choice.

"Brain training" exercises are another way to work on your cognitive fitness. Their purpose is to work on your short-term memory, processing skills, and so forth. There are even specific exercises to help with attention span. You will see some examples in Chapter 6 and Chapter 9, but chess, crossword puzzles, games, and even video games or games of skill like darts, bowling, or billiards can help hone your attention (Chia, 2021).

Word games have an obvious double-whammy. The more your brain is thinking about words, the more sensitized your mind is to words and the easier it will be to form reading habits or recognize words faster.

You might even notice reading becoming more significant in your life when you start doing things because they are *related* to reading. If you do crosswords initially because you want to improve your vocabulary and your recognition speed when you encounter a word, you may eventually find that you just enjoy spending time doing crossword puzzles. But the feeling of enjoyment is indirectly connected to your reading progress as well. This is one of the reasons that when things seem to be going well, they seem to be getting better faster!

Take Mental Breaks

Everybody will suffer from burnout eventually. Your attention span has a finite limit. Even if it didn't, your bladder does, and you will have to stop reading to use the washroom at some point! But your mind benefits from some break time in the same way that your eyes do. If you're following the 20-20-20 rule and stopping every 20 minutes to look at something 20 feet away for 20 seconds, then you should let your brain have a rest too.

Just as your brain will stop paying attention to continuous sounds, you will also stop paying attention to continuous inputs. Believe it or not, if you spend too long reading, your brain will just stop paying attention (Chia, 2021). So you should have a good rest, clear your mind, rest your eyes, stretch, and maybe take a short walk. The gains you get by "powering through" are offset by the losses in concentration, so you will make better progress in the long run by stopping occasionally.

More importantly, use the time to process what you have read. This is a great time to mentally review what you've just read and quiz yourself about the material. Try explaining it to yourself or pretend you're teaching it to someone else—even if there's no one to actually teach it to.

Having to explain something you have just learned is a very effective way to improve retention, but doing it when you stop occasionally is also very efficient. You get the benefit of relaxing your "reading muscles" for a few minutes, but you can still use the time to work on the material.

Does it seem like you are being told to concentrate, eliminate distractions, and stay on task on the one hand, and then immediately you are being told to stop, pause, relax, and not to push? In a way, that's true, but the real message is that you have to learn how to *balance* these things.

Imagine you are driving down a city street with timed lights. If you go too slow, your trip will take a long time anyway, but you'll also end up hitting all the traffic lights and it will take even longer. Similarly, if you go too fast, dodging and weaving through traffic, you just end up being the first car that gets to stop at the next red light—and prolonging your trip. But if you keep motoring along steadily at the speed the lights are set for, you effortlessly get there in the most efficient way possible.

This is what you need to do for your brain. Focus intently so that you don't get left behind and hit all the lights, but don't try to go so fast for so long that you wear yourself out. Moderation and continuous, gradual improvement are the keys.

Set a Time Limit

In order to control fatigue, taking occasional short breaks is very helpful, but there is also the longer-term buildup of fatigue that will affect you. For this reason, you should plan to set a time limit on your reading or training. Think of it like a football game: You have a break every quarter, but the game can't go on like that all night. Eventually, it's over.

How long you read or practice is going to depend on two things. First, there is your own schedule—appointments, other commitments, meal times, and so forth. You have to schedule your reading as though it were an appointment, which might determine how much time you can spend doing it. If you have to do something else that limits you to a half hour of reading, then you know what you have to work with.

The other thing that determines the length of your sessions is your own stamina. Don't set the length of the session by how much you have to read; set it by how long you can read before you start getting tired or losing concentration. If you keep going, you may find you have to do all that work over again anyway.

You should start small and try increasing the length of your sessions gradually. A good starting place is 20 minutes with a short break every five minutes. You could try increasing it by one minute every day. Whether this is too long or too short for you initially is something you will have to judge.

It's important to set a limit and stick to it. Not only does this keep your eyes and your brain from becoming fatigued, but it also makes being disciplined a habit. You will find that, with practice, not only does it become easier to form habits, but forming habits can become habit-forming!

If you do start to feel burnt out, then maybe it's time to try another task for a while. Don't linger and pretend to be reading either. Stop and fully switch tasks for a few minutes until you feel refreshed, then you might be able to return to reading with a second wind.

Don't worry about being productive either—the other task doesn't have to be a chore or useful. Playing a game on your phone or taking a short walk are great ideas. The idea is more like having a coffee break or giving children a 15-minute recess on the playground. Afterward, you can return refreshed, ready to knuckle down again for a little longer.

Your Body and Mind Affect Each Other

As you read in Chapter 4, eye fatigue can lead to general health problems, as can mental fatigue. If you try to read an entire novel in one sitting, you may find that you are just as worn out and unable to do things that evening as if you had been out all day digging ditches in the hot sun. But it works in the other direction as well.

Taking care of your body is an important step in allowing your mind to work at its full potential. If you haven't had enough sleep, you either won't be able to stay awake to read, or you won't be able to concentrate. If you aren't getting enough to eat, it can show up in your mental performance—you forget things, can't concentrate, get irritable. If you eat too much sugary food, you can experience dramatic changes in your glucose levels, which can make you drowsy (Chia, 2021).

When you are irritable, cues and cravings don't work the same way as when you're calm. Instead of being motivated to reach for a response that will satisfy your craving, you may get frustrated, lash out, or start looking around for other ways to make the craving go away rather than make the smart choice.

Exercise is beneficial to both your body and mind. The benefits of medium-intensity exercise on a regular basis include lowering stress and anxiety, keeping your cardiovascular system in good condition, and keeping your blood pressure in check. It can help maintain glucose levels. Exercise also promotes the release of brain-derived neurotrophic factor (BDNF), a chemical that has been shown to make memory work better (Harvard Health Publishing, 2013).

Summary

You have seen that there are a few things going on in the old noggin, some of them useful, and some of them not so useful. With a little planning and careful consideration, you should be able to strengthen the good stuff and get rid of the stuff that isn't helping.

Learning to read without using your inner voice will be an important step. Reading in larger phrases is important in terms of taking in more complete thoughts as one unit, not just finding bigger blocks of words with your eyes. You can train yourself to do this methodically.

You will have to work on getting rid of distractions, including those that come from the environment around you, as well as improving your own attention span and concentration. You will have to become devoted to reading. You have to learn to judge when the time is right to push on and when to stop and take a break. Working *too* hard can reach a point where it is counterproductive.

Finally, you have seen that the body and mind are not separate things. They are both part of *you*, and you will not perform at your peak in anything if they are not working in harmony. Taking care of your body will also help sharpen your mind, and that will help you improve your reading speed.

In the next chapter, the topic will be how to deal with the *information* you read—how to understand, or comprehend, it. I will also show you how better understanding leads to better speed. If you do it right, it will (at least appear to) work in reverse as well.

Chapter 6:
Comprehension

Decoding vs. Comprehension

When we read, there is a difference between simply decoding the material and comprehending it. Decoding is the process that occurs in the brain to make sense of the letters and turn them into words. Comprehension is a higher-level process in which you understand abstract meanings, process language, and so on.

There is an important language model developed by Gough and Tunmer that says that "Reading Comprehension (RC) is the product of Decoding (D) and Language Comprehension (LC) proficiencies" (Jiban, 2017). One way to interpret this is to say that if you can decode the symbols but don't understand the language, you won't have very good reading comprehension. As an example, you know all the letters in the French language (disregarding accents), but if you haven't learned French, it will be gibberish.

Similarly, if you know English very well but have trouble decoding, then you may have very poor reading comprehension because you can't turn the printed word into the language that you understand. This is common in people who have reading disabilities like dyslexia or are functionally illiterate—they get along just fine *speaking*, but there is a wiring problem that causes problems with the decoding portion of the process.

Decoding is the foundation on which reading is built. If you find that you have trouble in that regard, it is nothing to be ashamed of, and there are exercises that can help develop proficiency in decoding. Most of those techniques involve slowing down and going for accuracy. After you have the accuracy down, then it's time to work on speed.

Since you can't make up for trouble with decoding by using more language comprehension and vice versa, you definitely have to make sure both are strong. These make up the "core strength" of reading. The way to improve your language comprehension involves working on your vocabulary and general knowledge (Jiban, 2019). Further information on specific exercises will be given in Chapter 9.

Does Reading Faster Reduce Comprehension?

A common belief is that if you read too fast, you won't understand any of it. That's true if you don't read effectively, and for anybody, there is a limit to how fast they can process what they read. But if the question is posed as "Does reading faster *always* reduce comprehension?" then the answer is simply, "No."

The University of Chicago used to advise students that practicing reading more quickly for 10 minutes a day could improve their comprehension (2018). Kim Peak was a man who could read over 4,000 words per minute and had supposedly memorized 12,000 books (Vanderlinde, 2018). Mr. Peak was a special case and is in fact the person on whom the character Raymond was based in the movie *Rain Man* (Levinson, 1988).

Nobody expects to be able to learn to read like somebody who was neurodivergent, but the fact remains that it is *humanly* possible to read that fast and still comprehend. You're going after much more modest goals, so there is no reason to think you will have any less comprehension of what you read than anyone else.

You do want to make sure that you are not just working on speed, but that you are working on comprehension as well. You should include some checks on comprehension when you are building your training program. If you find that your comprehension is starting to slip, pay attention to *how* it's failing.

Bodybuilders don't only work on their arms and chest; every so often it's time to have "leg day." In the same vein, you may have to take a day off from working on speed and do some exercises on comprehension.

Reading for Comprehension

There is an excellent publication available for free online called *How to Read a Book* by Paul Edwards at the University of Michigan School of Information (n.d.). It can be retrieved from the web at pne.people.si.umich.edu/PDF/howtoread.pdf.

This guide is for academics and students who need to read nonfiction effectively with the highest degree of comprehension. It is not specifically concerned with speed, but almost every technique it mentions can be used to your advantage in both speed and comprehension.

For the most part, Edwards advises you to map out a strategy when you're reading. He makes 11 points. Here are the most important (n.d.):

- Have a purpose and strategy: State your goal and have steps mapped out that will lead you through the material to achieve that goal when you start a reading project of any size.

- Decide how much time you will spend: Consciously allocate your time based on your availability to each item you have to read.

- Focus on parts with high information content: Spend more time on things with lots of information. The table of contents can give you a lot of insight into the overall structure. Use charts and graphs to guide you to the paragraphs that are necessary to get details and spend less time on "filler" material.

- Use your unconscious mind: Like the advice you have received to take breaks and process what you've read, Edwards also says to let your mind "chew on" what you've read in between reading sessions.

The other things that he suggests are higher-level functions in an academic context, like being aware of who the authors are, whether they are part of an academic debate between competing theories, and what biases are present, for example. All these sorts of things have comparable ideas in other fields besides academia.

Really, the lesson to take away is that reading comprehension is a matter of relating the material you are reading to other things you already know. The more you know, the easier it is to do that, so the more you pay attention to the world around you, the better your comprehension will be—and not just when reading!

Previewing

Previewing is a great way to set yourself up for success in reading quickly while still understanding what you read. Think of it as reading a road map to learn your route before you launch yourself into an unexplored country. Instead of just putting your head down and diving into the details, you should try and get a sense of the main idea (Cain, 2022). As Edwards says, you should look at the table of contents and main headings. Take a look at this book, for example. If you haven't already, see what is coming up for the rest of this chapter and the following chapters. It will make things more familiar, and your mind will be more prepared to accept the information when it has a rough idea of what is coming.

If the text you're reading isn't well organized, or maybe it's not long enough to have a lot of headings and structure, then you can make use of skimming and scanning in order to get the gist of what each paragraph is about. The next section will cover those in more detail. Getting familiar with the structure and layout of an article or book is worth a couple of minutes of your time so that when you are actually reading, you know where you are.

The basic strategy here is to have a structure already set up in your mind so that when you read a detail, you have a place to put it. The human brain is really good at keeping track of connections between things. When you can't remember a fact or detail, it's usually because it's not connected to anything you already know. This is why so many memory techniques are systems to associate a fact—names, numbers, whatever—with something else.

Skimming and Scanning vs. Speed Reading

You have probably heard of skimming and scanning. Many people think that if someone is reading quickly, they are not reading all the material. That's the difference between speed reading and skimming or scanning. In speed reading, you *do* read every word. When you skim or scan something you don't read everything.

None of them is cheating, but all three techniques serve different purposes. You can use skimming and scanning to help you prepare for speed reading very effectively. They are very useful when developing your strategy. You can preview using both of them, and it will make your speed reading faster.

Skimming is not reading every word. A good example of skimming, and one that is recommended, is to read the first and last lines of each paragraph but skip over the text in the middle. This particular trick makes use of the fact that often in nonfiction writing, authors will introduce the idea of a paragraph, write supporting details, and end with a summarizing idea or a segue into the next paragraph.

By reading the first and last lines, you will have enough information in your mind to understand the overall structure of the document, and you will know what topics are going to be covered. You can then make another pass over it to get the details (Nowak, 2022).

Scanning is a bit different. In this case, scanning a document doesn't mean putting a copy of it onto your computer! It means looking it over, but it's more like trying to find your car in a parking lot. When you scan, you are looking for keywords. This is more appropriate when you already have an idea of what you're reading. An example would be a status report on a project—you might already know what teams are involved and what they are doing at each stage, so you might just be able to scan it for words like "on time," "without delay," "over budget," or "complications."

Going back to the idea of setting out to read with a goal and a strategy, that is the point when you should decide what you're going to be doing. So if you have to read a whole textbook, you will want to split it up into sessions, skim first, then go back and read for speed and comprehension. If you have to read an updated list of regulations, you might decide to just scan it and pay attention to the changes. Setting your goal will help determine which technique or combination of techniques is the best choice for the situation.

Recall & Review

You know that putting information into memory is important, but recalling it helps both with improving your comprehension and with making sure it moves from your short-term memory to your long-term memory. When you stop and take a break from reading is the perfect time to spend a moment recalling what you just read.

Taking notes is a good idea. They don't have to be a transcription of what you just read; just the main points will do. If you come across a fact that you find particularly interesting, jot it down. If there's something you think will prove to be very important later, make a note.

One of the other parts of improving comprehension is to read actively (Edwards, n.d.). Taking notes is one way to do that. Quizzing yourself or even explaining it back to yourself is another. Answering questions such as "who, what, where, when, and why?" serves to cement the information in your brain and develop associations with it (Cain, 2022).

To help with longer-term memory, you can also take a second round of notes at the end of your reading session. Don't try and rewrite the notes you put down during your breaks, though. Instead, try to make an overview, summary, or table of contents of the notes you already took.

Again, you have to balance a few things that seem to be contradictory. On the one hand, you are being told that you want to try and read things only once in order to do the fastest reading you can. On the other hand, you are being told to scan, read, write, and write again—all ways of processing the information over and over.

Yes, on one level, these do contradict each other. But when you get everything working together like a well-oiled machine, you will find that the net result is an increase in speed as well as quality. The time it takes to acquire the information is reduced because you are reading more efficiently.

The time you are spending sorting the information, organizing it, and comprehending it slows you down a bit, but you will get faster at it. And most importantly, it will be offset by all the time you would have spent rereading something because it didn't stick!

Information vs. Misinformation

These days, more than ever, it is crucial that you can not only read and understand things but that you are able to judge whether what you have read is true. You don't want to learn to read quickly with high comprehension only to have bought into an urban legend, or worse, to have helped it spread.

There are lots of conspiracy theories these days, and with more ways to communicate on the internet and through social media, you really have to keep your guard up. There are the old classics, like Elvis still being alive or that the moon landing was a hoax, but there are people who are *actively* trying to deceive others (Radford, 2008).

One notorious example is that Vladimir Putin and the Russian intelligence agencies have had well-developed propaganda and misinformation programs since the Cold War era. They have taken advantage of modern technologies, and according to a RAND Corporation report, "Russia seems to have enjoyed some success under its contemporary propaganda model, either through more direct persuasion and influence, or engaging in obfuscation, confusion, and the disruption or diminution of truthful reporting and messaging" (Paul & Matthews, 2016).

Another problem at the time of writing that seems about to explode is content generated by artificial intelligence (AI). Computers can scan the internet for writing on a number of topics, and they have been programmed to stitch it together in ways that seem coherent. The problem is that they don't actually *create* anything—making them highly likely to plagiarize—and they aren't able to apply any wisdom in choosing good information (Kelly, 2023). If there are numerous sites on the net about chemtrails, for example, AI content generators will often take them at face value and continue to propagate another myth told by those who are ignorant of science.

When you review something you have read, there are some other questions you should ask to help judge whether or not it is credible information, wrong information (misinformation), or the worst of the lot, disinformation ("fake news"). The International Federation of Library Associations and Institutions has recommended the following strategies for identifying fake news (2017):

- Consider the source. See who has written it and what organization has published the material. Do they have a bias?

- Who is the author? See if they are a real person and if they are credible.

- How old is it? Some things, like basic laws of physics, aren't going to change much, but current events often change from day to day.

- Kick the tires. Have you read a crazy headline designed to get your attention? What are the facts behind it? How much more to the story is there?

- Check the sources: If there are sources or links, follow up on them. In the worst case, they could be fakes, or they might be a pool of circular links just quoting each other with no basis in fact. Or they might be credible. Check them out.

- Is it serious? Maybe it's satire you're looking at. Double-check the source, and make sure it wasn't published on April 1.

- Ask the experts. When someone has spent years and years working in a field, they aren't doing it to take over the world as part of a dastardly plot. Rather, they probably know what they're talking about more than a random blogger.

- Check your bias. If anyone else told you the same thing you just read, would you believe them? Is there anyone you would believe it from? Maybe the problem is not what you're reading, but that maybe you have a blind spot you haven't been aware of. Check and make sure.

That's a lot to do, and there's no way that you should be expected to consider all of it every time you stop to rest your eyes! But you might keep track of a little "truth-o-meter" mentally so that when you reach the end, you have given some conscious thought to how valuable the information is.

Make sure that what you read is at least consistent with itself. After you read it but before you accept it as true, you can make sure it's consistent with other sources. Then you can decide, rationally, whether to keep it, throw it back, or if you need to look into the matter further.

Things You Shouldn't Speed Read

It was pointed out in the introduction that speed reading isn't a magic bullet. Not only that, but even if you get good at it, there are some things that you just *shouldn't* try and read fast. This comes down to the difference between knowledge and wisdom. There is an old saying: "Knowledge is understanding that a tomato is a fruit, but wisdom is not putting it in a fruit salad."

If you have been working on your speed and comprehension, it's natural to want to use your skills. But if you are reading an important legal document, it's not a good idea to speed read it. Legal documents are often written in language that, it could be argued, isn't even regular English. They are rife with terms and special usage, even bits of Latin.

If you misunderstand a legal document, you could be signing away rights or agreeing to terms that make you financially obligated now or in the future. The stakes are possibly quite high. Not only should you not speed read legal documents for this reason, but it's also often advisable to have a lawyer read them *for* you!

For the same reasons, medical documents, real estate contracts, and exam papers are bad choices for applying speed reading techniques. It might be fine to use speed reading when studying material for a class, but when you get to the actual exam, it's better to take your time and read the questions carefully. Many points are lost by students who read a question too quickly and don't answer what it is really asking.

Other things that are not good candidates for speed reading can be very technical documents, computer programs, mathematics, and large lists of data. In these cases where the language is very specialized and the content is very dense, it takes a different sort of mental processing to be sure that accuracy is given the highest priority. You may be able to read them faster than you could before you learned speed reading, but you shouldn't push yourself.

Summary

This chapter has quite a few things for you to chew on. Reading quickly isn't the only important thing you have to learn to do. You have to make sense of it, understand it, and retain it. If you are slow at that part, it doesn't matter how quickly you can look at the words.

You now understand that reading comprehension comes from decoding the symbols on a page combined with understanding the language they represent. You know that it's possible to increase both your comprehension and your reading speed. You need to have a purpose and strategy when you sit down to read.

You also want to stack the deck in your favor by previewing the reading material as much as possible before you start. Having a good understanding of the outline of the text lets you form a mental frame so that you have a place to hang the information you are taking in. Then repeating it, recalling it, or even writing down notes after the fact can help move that information into your long-term memory.

All of this shows that there is more to reading than just sitting down and flipping through the pages in front of you. You have to think about *what* you're reading, and you have to think about *how* you're reading. In the next chapter, you'll see some more new approaches.

Chapter 7:
Think Different

This chapter is a refrain. It's where you can take the opportunity to reconsider some of the information from previous chapters and reflect on those topics. Speed reading has a different place in your life; it is something that requires focus and commitment while you are doing it. For some people—most notably, those who already read a lot—it can be really hard to change some of those habits, so that's the reason for tying things together here.

Take Reading Seriously

You have heard this part of the message before, but there's a difference between reading effectively and holding a book so that you look cool down at the coffeehouse. When you're reading as an information-processing activity, you want to avoid noise and distractions. You want to make a clear space where you can concentrate. You want to fully immerse yourself in reading.

You need to make your reading time sacred—both in terms of how you respect it and how you expect others to respect it. You should not schedule activities during the time you have set aside for training. You should schedule reading time as if it's an appointment during which you can't be disturbed. This also helps you determine your time limit for your reading sessions.

Furthermore, if someone asks you to read something and you say you will do it, treat that as a promise. Don't say, "Oh, sure, when I get the chance, I'll give it a look," and then not make it a priority. The reason for saying this is not because anyone is judging you for how well you keep your word. (That's important, but that is between you and your conscience!)

The reason to make reading commitments important is that doing so affects your own attitude toward reading. You want to make reading something *real*, something *attractive*, something *valuable*. Not getting around to doing something is a sign that it's not that important to you. Actions speak louder than words, after all. So if you treat reading as a privilege rather than an obligation, it will make so much difference in your progress.

Think Actively About Reading

You have to treat reading as an important activity when you're not doing it by doing things like making a place for it in your day and in your home or office. But that's not enough. You have to think about reading when you're not doing it as well as when you are in the middle of doing it. The most important thing to pay attention to is what kind of reading you're doing.

The type of reading will make a difference. If you're reading emails and correspondence, you won't need to do the same amount of previewing as you would for a longer text, but it's still important to note what's going on. The main points in an email are often found in the middle of the text, after pleasantries and greetings. Take all the rules you learned about writing business letters—the customs everybody is supposed to use— and use that information to your advantage in knowing where the meat of the message will be found.

Specific techniques for reading on electronic devices will be discussed in Chapter 8, but remember that you can use pacers and trackers to help you blast through emails quickly. Skimming and scanning might even be possible, especially when you are faced with a one-sentence message that has four paragraphs of corporate disclaimers and privacy statements—no need to read all that!

Magazines, newspapers, and periodicals are often highly organized for you. You'll be able to see headings or pick out topic sentences (Ostrov, 2002). You should be aware that some popular publications are written to capture your attention and that whatever editorial policies they use will cause some sort of bias. When reviewing and thinking about the material, it's worthwhile to note if there is any particular slant, whether it's obvious or more subtle.

If you're reading longer reports, it will be helpful to do more previewing. Make a plan for when you're going to read, how long you're going to read, where you're going to read, and so forth. Ask yourself if the material is something you can go over quickly, or if it's something you really need to study in-depth.

Another very important thing to realize is that there is a difference between being *fast* and being *in a hurry*. Being fast is your goal, and that's a good thing. Being in a hurry is to be avoided. When you're in a hurry, you're not living in the moment, and you're not focused on the thing in front of you. What you're actually paying attention to is the *next* thing you want to do, with results that range from disappointing to disastrous.

When you try to do things in a hurry, you make mistakes. You get sloppy. It can actually end up being slower trying to go fast because you have to go back and read something over again. Your accuracy and comprehension suffer. Don't rush. The trick is to be fast but relaxed. You should be reading quickly and effortlessly. Pushing yourself is for training. The advice here is, "Never be in a hurry."

Training

This isn't the first time we've made a distinction between reading and training to read in this book, but it's a good time to clarify what that means. It's a lot like running or doing any other sport. Before you go for a run, you stretch. Before you enter a marathon, you train. You work on speed, strength, and stamina.

It's the same for speed reading. Chapter 9 is where you will find suggestions for exercises and drills. Right now, the point to make is that you need to schedule time for training. This is the most burdensome part of improving your reading speed, the part that is the most like a chore, and the reason why you need to develop training as a habit using the techniques from Chapter 2.

When it comes to training, the *most* important thing is to do it regularly. Training does not have to, nor should it, be lengthy and difficult. You do not have to find a two-hour block of time in the middle of your day to train effectively. On the contrary, frequent but small exercises are far more effective. In fact, you can flip the notion of taking breaks on its head and use breaks from other activities as chances to train.

Of course, if you are doing something visually intensive like driving, reading when you want to rest your eyes is not the best choice. But if you're spending the morning in meetings and have a 15-minute break, you could do five or 10 minutes of reading drills.

When you're actually reading, you're going for speed, but when you are training, you're working on speed (Ostrov, 2002). Timed readings and eye exercises are important, and you need to make sure you are doing these training sessions every day.

Set aside a few times in the day—perhaps just after breakfast, after lunch, and after dinner—to do a few reading drills. Record your times and notes in your phone or a small notebook you carry with you. If you find yourself waiting for an appointment, add a bonus five-minute reading workout. This is much more effective and makes training a lot more fun than feeling like you have to bolt in for a two-hour workout.

Reading for Pleasure

If you're reading for pleasure, you get to choose how to enjoy yourself. It's alright to relax and take things easy. You might prefer to use some of the speed techniques anyway, but it's not going to undo all your progress if you don't. Previewing a murder mystery might defeat the purpose by giving away the end! Some people prefer not to let anything interfere with the formation of new habits, so they might prefer to stay in speed reading mode all the time. If you're reading for pleasure, the choice is yours.

When you do return to training, notice whether it's easier to read fast. Is there any difference in your speed? Your comprehension? It's unlikely to be a big difference. Don't worry about small changes—one or two words a minute are within normal variations anyway. But if for some reason you do see a significant difference, then be a little stricter about your methods until they are better established. After you have been speed reading for 20 years, it will become automatic.

Letting go and having a "free" reading session can help with your speed reading skills because it is a chance to get more positive feedback from the act of reading. Getting lost in a page-turner is fun, and anything that associates reading with fun is worthwhile. You might have a flashback to the campaign to promote literacy, "Reading is FUNdamental!" The program can be found online at www.rif.org.

With this in mind, you have to again make a conscious decision about what you want to accomplish when you read. It may be to simply let yourself be transported away by a good story, and if that's the case, then you *want* to just soak in the imagery. But be clear about what you're doing and why. Realize that "work reading" and "play reading" are completely different activities and should be done differently. Driving a car is one thing, but Formula 1 takes an entirely different skill set than running down to the shopping center through school zones!

Your State of Mind

What is your state of mind? Are you calm? Distracted? Preoccupied? Do you have an open mind? Are you panicked or upset? How you are doing will have an effect on your performance in almost any activity, and that most certainly includes reading.

A study conducted in 2012 found that 94% of the people surveyed reported that, of 18 different states of mind, being calm, happy, and energized were the three linked to the best performance and effectiveness (Caillet et al., 2014). Those 18 states of mind are listed here, roughly split into positive and negative states:

Negative	Positive
• stressed	• content
• tired	• calm
• anxious	• satisfied
• frustrated	• excited
• disappointed	• energized
• angry	• happy
• depressed	• euphoric
• hopeless	• ecstatic
• desperate	• elated

If you are in a depressed state, then it is wise to seek professional help or contact the 988 hotline. But if you are experiencing any of the items in the left-hand column, it wouldn't be the least surprising if you were having difficulty concentrating or reading effectively. Even just a bad night's sleep or not having your usual morning coffee can cause you to slow down. If any of these negative feelings persist, again, you should seek professional help. But let's talk about a couple of ways you can help keep yourself from letting things get out of control.

The first thing is to make sure you are well-rested. Yes, there are times when you have to push through to meet a deadline, but it will come at the expense of quality or your health. Take time off; even a catnap can help. Come back in the morning when you're fresh.

If you can put what you're feeling into words, it can help make those feelings seem less urgent and become more abstract. Verbalizing takes the problem away from your inner emotional self and gives it to your rational adult brain. Exerting control is harder when you're stressed or anxious, so it's even more important to stop, take a deep breath, and try to find a little sense of calm.

Exercise has been shown to help reduce stress, so a quick visit to the gym or even a walk around the block can help iron out some of the wrinkles in your day. Likewise, make sure you are eating well, including regular meals and a balanced diet. It is far too easy to forget to take care of yourself when you are trying to kill a dragon, but all the dragon has to do is wait for you to tire yourself out.

The last thing you should keep track of is how open-minded you are. Are you approaching your reading material with a chip on your shoulder, thinking that it's not going to tell you anything you don't already know? If so, why bother picking up that book? You should be looking forward to it with a sense of curiosity about what you might discover.

Even if it's a topic you know well, you never know when you'll add a new viewpoint to your understanding of the subject. And if you get through it and find nothing new, remember that sometimes it's nice to have a refresher and verify that nothing changed while you weren't looking.

Previewing

You've learned about previewing, and you know a few different ways to approach it. But there's one more point to consider about previewing what you're reading: how it affects your attitude. You have better odds of achieving your goals when you have thought about what they are and make reading a premeditated act.

By previewing, you make up a little list of "to-do" items that you will check off along the way. You will get a sense of the structure and main points of the text and feel a sense of accomplishment as you check them off your list. By thinking about reading as a small project with several aspects that need to be addressed in order to complete it, it becomes harder to stay aloof and unengaged.

Don't Multitask

Are you counting how many times this idea is repeated? Are you going to hear it again? Yes, yes, a thousand times yes! Multitasking is the enemy of the speed reader.

You are looking to find a place of calm, centered focus. Multitasking is exciting, divided, and stressful. You can't read and multitask. In fact, research has shown for nearly 10 years that you can't really multitask anyway (Napier, 2014). Stop trying. Get back to those books!

Summary

In addition to learning some techniques, your good attitude is one of the key things you should try and bring to your reading. Make it important. Train diligently, read seriously, and don't forget to have some fun with it. It's an interesting thing to do—gleaning knowledge that has been impressed upon a dead tree or radiated from a screen! Don't forget how wonderful that can be.

Speaking of screens, the next chapter is where you will learn about some particular techniques that can be used when you're reading on a computer or tablet. It's time to look at speed reading for the 21st century.

Chapter 8:
Speed Reading for Screens

Reading on a Screen Is Different

Reading has changed a lot since the mass adoption of the personal computer and even more since the turn of the century. The internet, smartphones, tablets, smart TVs—all these devices are used to show us words where we used to read books and newspapers.

Reading on a screen differs in a couple of ways from reading so-called "physical" media. Screens are a different format, and the way we approach them physically is different. When you read on a computer or laptop, the screen is oriented vertically, or mostly vertically. It is usually further away, either because a desktop monitor sits at the back of the desk or because a laptop is often held on our lap; in the case of a desktop, the text is higher than usual, and with a laptop, it is lower.

But the differences are more than ergonomic. People who read things digitally tend to be overconfident in their reading comprehension (Benson, 2020). Research shows that understanding headings and getting the main idea of a piece read digitally is not a problem, but that details can be missed, and comprehension suffers when people read long pieces (Singer & Alexander, 2016).

Scrolling is a very different process for our eyes. You have heard about using the technique of previewing to build a mental framework of the text. Some research shows that it is more difficult to do this when the material is presented in a scrolling format (Hou et al., 2017). One theory is that the moving text is processed differently by the brain—the visual system is very sensitive to motion.

Whatever the reason, there are some things that you will be better able to read on paper. It also seems that involving the hands and making reading a tactile experience affects comprehension. Since one of the methods used to increase comprehension is to involve more than one sense, that also makes sense. There is less interaction with a screen than with paper books or newspapers.

This is not to say that you shouldn't read on a screen. For one, it's likely going to be impossible to avoid it entirely. You don't want to be seen as a Luddite and walking environmental disaster by being the lone person asking for a printed copy when everybody else is happy to get the electronic version in their email. Sometimes the convenience of having access to a lot of information without having to carry bulky books is worth the trade-off.

Being aware of the tendency to gloss over material when reading electronic media is half the battle to fixing the problem. Since you are going to be planning your reading and reading actively, you will just add one more item to your checklist. If you are reading denser material on a screen, take more time in reviewing when you pause for breaks. Keeping notes physically and writing them longhand with a pencil can involve other parts of your brain and give you a better grip on any ideas that are "slippery."

Brightness & Eye Fatigue

In Chapter 4, we talked about the role brightness and lighting play in causing eye strain. Taking a break every 20 minutes is still necessary, and adjusting the brightness of the screen is important. You may or may not have as much control over the ambient lighting conditions if you are mobile, on public transportation, or outdoors, but that doesn't mean you are completely powerless.

You can choose where to sit. If there is a shaded area, take advantage of it so you do not have to read in bright sunlight. If you are in an area that is too dark, remember that your eyes find it easier to pay attention if the screen isn't the brightest thing you are looking at. There's no exact setting number that is perfect, and what one person considers excellent might be difficult for someone else to use. The best approach is to set the brightness and contrast to the lowest setting that you can comfortably read. Pay attention and adjust accordingly, but if you find yourself peering at the screen or squinting, you've probably gone too far.

You can often adjust the theme of your browser or screen. Instead of dark text on a light background, it might be easier to use a dark theme. The light text on a dark screen reduces the overall brightness if you are in a place where you can't turn up the room lights. (Don't be that person who thinks other people won't notice you reading in a movie theater, though!)

If your eyes feel dry and tired, try to blink more frequently in addition to taking regular breaks. Incorporate a blink into your training regimen. Trying to blink when you reach the end of each line is probably going to make you feel like you're reading under a strobe light—especially as your reading speed increases—but every paragraph or five to six lines might be good. Combine that with counting the lines as you read them, and you can kill two birds with the same stone—remembering to blink and stop subvocalizing.

Blinking helps keep your eyes moist, but if that doesn't work, you can use artificial tears. Over-the-counter (nonprescription) artificial tears can be purchased at most pharmacies. You should not use ones that say they have a "redness remover," because those can make dry eyes worse (Mayo Clinic, 2022b).

If you wear glasses, there are lens coatings that can prevent glare as well. Your optometrist is a good source of information. If you wear bifocals, you can get different arrangements of the prescriptions that are optimized for computer work or close work. If you don't wear glasses, again, you should still consider getting your eyes checked once a year and any time you have difficulty reading, such as if you experience headaches, fatigue, or other symptoms.

Be aware that using polarized sunglasses while trying to read a screen can result in it either being perfectly visible or looking like it's completely dark, especially with liquid crystal displays (LCD). This is a result of the screen emitting light that's already polarized in one direction. As long as your glasses are close to the same polarization, it will work fine, but if you turn the screen sideways, it might not work at all. (It's a neat parlor trick if you have friends who haven't seen it before.)

Adjust Text Size & Format

There are a couple of things you can do when reading on a screen that are obviously difficult any other way. You can increase the size of the type so that it's comfortable. There is a balance between making it large enough to be clear and being able to fit a lot of information on the screen.

You can also adjust the spacing between lines on many screen-reading apps and tablets. You will find that single-spaced text is often a bit cluttered. Double-spaced text, like a lot of legal documents, seems a bit unnatural—though on paper, it's great for making notes right by the text. Try a few timed readings, as described in Chapter 9, and see what works best for you using solid measurements rather than just how it "feels." But if it doesn't feel okay, no matter what the numbers say, then make a change! Comfort is key.

You can also adjust the typeface (font) and choose the foreground and background colors. Some colors may seem easier to read. Ironically, using sepia tones that look older and warmer can make using digital devices more "palatable" to the eye (*Speed Reading on Screens*, 2021). Generally, you're looking for neutral, pale colors that still contrast with the text.

In cases where you find a page of information that is poorly laid out or cluttered with images or unrelated ads, it might be worth your while to copy the text and paste it into a word processor or text editor (*Speed Reading Methods*, 2010). You don't want to have to spend your day doing layout and desktop publishing just to read something, but it's important to remember that you have control. If you want something to look different, by all means, copy the text and ditch the ads. If it's formatted in wide columns, you can resize the columns to be narrower and allow you to make fewer fixations.

Many books or ebooks are formatted with what is known as "full justification," which is when extra space is inserted between letters and words so that the right-hand margin comes out even. This makes for a page of text that looks pretty from a distance, but it is a case of putting style over substance. The space between words becomes variable in order to make the right edge of each line even, so your brain has to constantly adjust in order to *find* the next word.

Text that is left-justified, where the left margin looks even but the right margin is uneven, is much easier to read. It allows the spacing to remain constant, following rules that typesetters have had 500 years to perfect since the invention of the printing press. If you have the ability to do so, you can simply "select all" and left-justify the entire document before you read it.

You might also be able to use serial viewer software, which I will discuss just a few paragraphs from now, to present the information in a very fast and specialized way. Computers are not just capable of displaying text for you to read, but you have a lot of power over changing the form in which it is presented.

One caveat: Don't get lost in reformatting and adjusting things. This is the same trap as when someone sits down to work at their desk and ends up shuffling all their papers or rearranging their furniture so they can "get comfortable to work." You have to be aware of when you're making a change that will pay off in terms of reading productivity and when you are actually just procrastinating.

The first few times you try and do something a different way, there will naturally be adjustments to make. When you make them, write down what you like or save your settings so that your future self won't have to spend time choosing a type size and brightness setting all over again. Even if it needs to be adjusted, you will speed yourself up by already having a starting point.

Pacers on a Screen

You have a lot of options for pacers and trackers when you read on a screen. You wouldn't want to use your finger on a screen because you will leave grease marks. You don't want to be the person in the old "blonde" joke: "How can you tell when the blonde has been using the word processor? There's white-out on the screen." Of course, blondes don't have a monopoly on being silly, but you don't want to smear things on the screen.

This is also a good time to remember that in addition to making sure your eyes are in good shape and that your glasses are clean, you should keep your screens clean as well. Don't let them accumulate dust and grime. Use a soft, non-scratchy cloth, and if you need to moisten it, wet the cloth instead of spraying any cleaner directly on the screen. Check your manufacturer's directions for any special cleaning instructions.

You can use the cursor as a tracker, or you can use highlighting in some programs. Just follow along with the text using the cursor as you would with your finger. How well this works for you may depend on the kind of mouse you have and how comfortable you are while using it (*Speed Reading Methods*, 2010).

Read-only mode is a good idea if you're highlighting or working in a word processor so you don't end up deleting pieces or editing documents that you didn't intend to change. Another idea would be to make a "reading copy" of the file and keep the original unchanged. This is not a bad idea if you want to make notes in your own copy of the document anyway.

One way to adapt your usual techniques of speed reading to the screen is to use a window as a "virtual card." Instead of using a card or piece of paper to cover the text above the line that you are reading, you can use the edge of the window or the top of the screen to cover the text. You aren't really covering it, it's actually just scrolling up past the window or screen, but it's the same effect.

Not having to turn pages can save you a little time. If you are using the top edge of your window as a tracker, you can just keep scrolling steadily. Some mice and computers will let you set an auto-scroll. In most web browsers, if you put the cursor in the middle of the page and click the middle button or mouse wheel, you will see a different cursor. At this time, moving the mouse up or down will make the page automatically scroll. There are external packages and plug-ins for browsers that will add auto-scroll features to your web browser. "Autoscroll" is the name of one that has been around since 2008 (Snyder, 2019).

With auto-scroll, you can control the speed by how far away from the center of the screen you pull the mouse. If you move the wheel again or click on the motion cursor, it will go back to normal mode. Alternatively, you can continually scroll using the mouse wheel without activating the auto-scroll mode. Some people find it difficult to fixate on moving text though. If this describes you, then you might prefer to read a section of text and move by hitting the page down key.

On a tablet or similar device, sometimes the volume keys can be set to turn the page. This is faster than swiping because you can just leave your hand resting on the volume keys rather than having to move it to the touch screen. Choosing the best method for you isn't guesswork—measure your reading speed using several methods and use whichever shows the fastest results.

Small Screens

There are pros and cons to using a small screen like a phone. On the one hand, when you get to the point where you can use very few fixations to take in the information on a page, having a small screen greatly reduces the amount of text you have to work with. On the other hand, there is less room for other things that can distract your vision.

The format of a small screen forces all columns to be narrow. In fact, you can see the entire screen in your field of vision, so with practice, you might be able to read the whole screen at once. A book reader on a phone using the volume buttons to scroll can be very quick.

Don't be afraid to turn the phone or tablet into landscape mode if it makes more sense. If you want to use a larger text size, breaking the lines up into such short lines by using portrait mode may make it difficult for long words to be printed without being split. In landscape mode, you will be able to have more meaningful lines but fewer of them.

Just because a screen is small doesn't mean you have to hold it close to your eyes—in fact, you will be less likely to get eye strain if you hold the screen further back. Without an RSVP program to display the text, which I will explain in the next section, you will be limited by a small screen, but it isn't completely useless. Book-sized screens as you'd find on a tablet, say a 7-inch screen, can be excellent displays with all the advantages of electronic displays and a highly portable size.

RSVP

Reducing the number of saccades or jumps your eyes make between fixations is a key strategy to improving your reading speed. It's the mechanism that explains why narrow columns are easier to read. The narrowest column you could make would be one word long, but you would still have to move your eyes to scan down to read lines. What if you could eliminate moving your eyes completely?

This is the theory behind a technique known as rapid serial visual presentation, or RSVP. The definition of RSVP is "the process of sequentially displaying images at the same spatial location at high presentation rates," which are usually greater than 10 words per second (Lees et al., 2018). In other words, you just look at the same spot, and a computer displays the words you will read. It's like watching a movie of the words—it should be the one time the movie is exactly as good as the book!

While Lees et al. describe RSVP systems that use brain-computer interfaces (BCI) to control the speed of the words being displayed, this is the leading edge of research and has not left the laboratory—or at least not become affordable yet, despite the fact that it has been researched since the 1960s (2018). In 1992, experiments comparing how fast people could read text in paragraph form versus RSVP form found that with the same size letters, people jumped from 303 words per minute to 1,171 words per minute using RSVP (Rubin & Turano).

Further, they found that six of the 13 subjects tested were able to maintain comprehension scores of 75% or higher and read at the maximum rate the machinery was able to present text, which was 1,652 words per minute. Rubin and Turano concluded that saccades were definitely a limiting factor in how fast a reader can perform. Clearly, RSVP has some serious potential when it comes to improving speed by eliminating eye motion.

Yet it is still possible to get software that will let you use an ordinary device or computer to read via RSVP. For a sample, visit www.elvers.us/perception/rsvp/.

There are also software packages that you can purchase. Some of these are Spreeder, AceReader, 7 Speed Reading, and Reader's Edge. These range from $9 to over $100 (Bartels, 2023). Other options are free, such as web readers. Some features to look for include setting how fast they display the text, how many words to show you at once, and whether or not you can load your own material into them (Mark, 2021).

You can use AccelaReader's website (www.accelareader.com), and Spreeder also has a website (www.spreeder.com) that lets you paste text into a window. Both of these websites provide ways to try RSVP for yourself before you spend any money on it. There are other free packages out there, and an internet search will turn up the ones that are currently available for your devices.

Distractions

Focusing on reading is important, and some people find that using a computer or portable device is an aid in that regard. There are also many ways that computers and gadgets can be more distracting, especially when connected to the internet. In Chapter 5, you read that it's good practice to put your devices away when you're trying to read, but that really doesn't apply when you are reading *on* your device!

One of the best things you can do is use full-screen mode. This is commonly available in most text viewers. Adobe Acrobat Reader has a "Read Mode," which turns off extraneous menus, for example. You should also consider going to full-screen mode so that you can't be distracted by things you see in other windows.

If you have other programs that are constantly making noise and notifying you of every little thing that is happening, such as social media apps or email, then disabling the notifications is a no-brainer. Whether you need to adjust the settings for each application separately or just turn the sound off for your whole device is your choice, so do whatever works for you.

Remember that multitasking is okay for your computer to do, but not for *you* to do. It can be hard to realize that we're not focused on one task when we're seated at a screen. To an outside observer, it just looks like you're sitting there using a tablet or computer, and maybe it feels that way to you. But if you have three open windows and a video playing in the background, you're not paying full attention to any of them. (You were warned that you were going to hear this point over and over!)

It might even be worthwhile to have a separate device just for reading. Not so long ago, that would have seemed like a luxury or even an excess. These days, a tablet that is just for reading is something you might get for free with a cell phone plan, so it's not out of the realm of possibility. Having a device that only has reading software and files on it—no games, no social media apps—can help keep you on the straight and narrow when you're working on reading.

The other thing you can do to greatly reduce the temptations of the internet is disconnect your network cable or turn off your Wi-Fi or data. Download your reading material and go off-grid. It's hard to get lost down a rabbit hole on the web if you aren't connected.

Summary

This chapter showed you that using technology can give you a boost in training for speed reading. Ebooks and devices can make it easy to carry your reading material with you and let you use some strategies that just aren't available with paper media, like changing the formatting to be more efficient or even keeping your eyes perfectly still while using RSVP techniques.

At the same time, you have to be aware of what you're doing so that you can avoid pitfalls. You may need to compensate for increases in speed by working harder and smarter on your reading comprehension. There are distractions for us when we get lost in the computer, either by fussing with settings or by alarms and notifications.

You now have all the "book learning" you're going to need. The next, and final, chapter is where you can start putting what you've learned into practice.

Chapter 9:
Practice Tips and Exercises

You Have to Train

It's time to set theory aside and start doing the work. This is where you get busy. As mentioned earlier, there is a difference between training for a race and actually competing. Likewise, you have physical and mental reading skills that you want to be able to practice in a way where it's okay to make mistakes and where you can push yourself to improve.

Yes, all reading is good, but to specifically make progress at speed reading, you need to train regularly. How often? That will depend on your own goals. If you don't train every day, though, it will be difficult to make the habits stick effectively. The minimum requirement would be 15 minutes of training each day outside of any reading you do for work or pleasure.

More is better, up to a point. In Chapters 4 and 5, you learned that it's important to take mental and physical breaks. You can increase your time spent training every day, but you shouldn't do it all at once. You are going to make more progress in three sessions of 20 minutes than you will in one hour-long session. This also makes it easier to fit into your day.

When you are actually reading, you are more interested in the content so comprehension comes first. When you are training, the idea is to do speed drills and push to improve (Ostrov, 2002). Again, think of training like working on sprints at a football practice. It will get you in shape for the football game, but once you're in the football game, it doesn't matter how fast you can run if you drop the ball. You want to run fast *with* the ball.

Make a Space to Read

It's best to center yourself and read in a quiet space where you have room to work with your book and any guides. If you want to keep notes or times, then it's convenient to have space for a notepad and pen or whatever you use to record things. If your situation doesn't permit you to use a private office, try to at least find a quiet space where you can pay attention.

Soft music can be helpful. Headphones can help shut out the noisy world around you. Listening to music can help quiet your inner voice and stop subvocalizing. The tempo of the music can possibly be a tool to keep your pace while reading.

You need a certain amount of physical space, but even more important is the mental space you are in. Remember you need to be calm and not worried about anything. Whatever other concerns you have can wait for a few minutes until you are done with the task in front of you. Take a few deep breaths until you are fully relaxed and alert.

The important thing is that you establish your concentration and don't let anything external disturb it. If something or someone does disturb you, don't get agitated. As a doctor said to the patient with a kidney stone, "This, too, shall pass."

Measuring Your Speed

There is more than one way to measure how fast you read. You can have someone help you by operating a clock or stopwatch for you, leaving you free to concentrate on reading. You can use an online website if you want. One example can be found at www.freereadingtest.com, or a search of the internet will return some others. You may or may not be able to choose the text that you read, and that may become something you want to control. Most likely, you are going to be working solo anyway, so you should know how to measure your reading speed manually; this is also useful when your data connection has gone on the fritz.

The simplest way is to set a time limit, say one minute, and set a timer. If you have an actual stopwatch, that's not as useful on your own because you can't watch it while you're reading. The timer on your phone or microwave oven, or even just a kitchen timer, would be preferable.

Start the timer and read until it goes off. Stop immediately and mark the word. You can now count the words. This works but is fairly time-consuming. If you're reading in a word processor, you can highlight the selection you read and have the computer count it for you.

The truth is that the *exact* number of words per minute isn't that important. A variation of two, three, or even five percent faster or slower is not enough to get worried about. You might have picked a particular passage with unusual words or that was written poorly. There might have been a distracting noise outside that cost you some time during the timed session. The average is more important than any one score.

If the average person reads 250 words per minute (wpm), then 5% is 12 or 13 wpm. If another person has been practicing and is reading at a speed of 500 wpm, then 5% for them is 25 wpm. The person reading 250 wpm shouldn't feel bad if they got a one-time measurement as low as 238, and they shouldn't go around bragging about a one-time measurement of 262. The person who reads 500 wpm could be anywhere between 475 and 525 wpm. (The faster you get, the more leeway you have.)

The shorter your timing, the less representative it will be, but there are two approaches you can use to measure things better. One is to average out four or five short timings. Simply read for one minute, count the words up, and make a note of the total. After you have done this four times, average your scores.

The other way to be more accurate is to read for a longer period of time. If you read for four minutes, you should get a pretty close number to the average of four separate timings. If you read for 10 minutes, that's even better.

When you do a long timing, it gives you a measure of your stamina. It's easy to stay focused for just one minute, but staying "in the zone" for 10 minutes takes more effort. You will be challenged to face more internal and external distractions in a 10-minute timing than in a shorter one. In that sense, you can measure something with long timings that you can't with short ones. Both have their uses.

Counting every word that you read isn't always practical, and if we're allowing as much as +/- 5%, it's not even necessary. Instead, you can work out an average number of words per line. Once you know that, you can just count lines and multiply the number of lines by the average number of words.

The average number of letters in a word is considered to be five for most normal text. Medical or academic texts may be higher, but that's not the best material to choose for speed reading training. Choose a novel or some columnar text without too many pictures or inserts. Count the total number of *characters*—including letters, spaces, and punctuation marks. Divide the total by five, and that will be a pretty good average number of words per line (Beale & Mullan, 2008).

For example, the line above has 90 characters, so 90 divided by 5 is 18. Lo and behold, that line happens to have exactly 18 words! (You won't necessarily get that lucky, but it will be close.)

Another way to find the number of words per line is to count the number of words in five or 10 lines of print. Take the total number of words and divide by the number of lines. Round to the nearest whole number.

Again, a word here or there is nothing to quibble over. You are most interested in a reasonable average, and you're interested in *patterns*— whether your speed is improving overall and whether it is improving quickly or slowly. There's no real difference between reading 300 and 305 words per minute. There *is* a difference between 300 and 400 wpm. There's no real difference between increasing your speed by 1 wpm per week, but if that changes to improving by 1 wpm per *day*, then that's noteworthy!

Baseline & Keeping Records

If you're tracking progress, you will need to have a "before" picture to compare with your performance after you practice. So before you ever start speed reading, time yourself over, say, five pages of material. Just read it naturally, the way you would before you started this book.

You want to record this. Start a notebook or spreadsheet somewhere and do regular timings. You don't need to do them every time you read, however. Since it was just mentioned that you aren't worried about tiny changes, measuring your reading speed once or twice a week gives you a better sense of how you're doing than measuring three times a day. (That's just going to show you that you get sleepy after lunch!)

Advice is often given to dieters to do the same thing for the same reasons. A little variation day to day is normal, but if you see how much you weigh once a week, the numbers are much more meaningful.

It is a good idea to log your practice times. This will give you a record you can look back on, but it also motivates you to fill in the form every day, which helps to make practice a habitual ritual. You can keep as much information as you like. A logbook might look like this:

At the end of the week, you can write your timed reading speed. Recording it in the top corner of the right-hand page allows you to just flip through your notebook and quickly get an idea of how you are progressing.

You can keep track of more information about your reading if you like. You can keep it in a different format, with more columns. It's really up to you, but you don't want to get lost in record keeping. A simple format that you can remember is easier to jot down on the back of an envelope if you find yourself without your logbook.

Some Sample Exercises

Sprints

Here is a method you can use to help build your reading speed (University of Chicago, 2018). It involves reading some of the same text over and over, so it can get repetitive. You can use a book or several page-long articles—nonfiction is good so that you don't get too engrossed in the story. Find the average number of words per line and count the lines per page. It can be good to prepare some materials like this—getting averages for words and lines—but not necessarily use that material for this session. Build up a little pile of material that you will use for future sessions.

Pick a starting point and set a one-minute timer. Read at a comfortable pace, without hurrying. The second time, you will start at the *same* place and read for one minute, but this time you'll use a tracker. Use a finger, pen, or card—your choice. This time, push yourself and see if you can read twice as far.

Do it a third time and see if you can go three times as far. It's a good idea to stop and, before you figure out the speed, answer a few questions, especially the five Ws: who, what, where, when, and why? Make a note and maybe rate yourself from 1–5 on how well you feel you understood things.

After you have done this, pick a new starting place just after where you ended. If you need to read a little more to get to a logical starting place, such as the beginning of a paragraph or section, then go ahead. Now you can do another set of sprints.

You can determine the number of sprints to put into a set, and the number of sets to put into a practice session, but don't be surprised if 10 minutes tires you out. It's also okay that you're reading the same material over and over. You may say, "That's cheating—of course I'll read it faster the second or third time around." Yes, you will, and that's by design. The point is for you to get used to the *feeling* of reading faster. You will work on using your eyes and muscles faster. It really is a physical exercise.

Grouping

Visual Grouping

The first kind of practice is to expand your field of view. This is a necessary skill if you want to take in more than one word at a glance, which will reduce the number of saccades per line.

Don't even read at first. Just hold the book a few inches further from your eyes than usual or slide it back on the table. If you prefer, use a book holder, or put together a makeshift one, so that every line of text is the same distance away.

Now, focus on the word that is closest to the center of the page. Without moving your eyes, try and read the words that surround the central word; this is to help soften your gaze. You don't have to make sense of the page, just try and read all the words that are adjacent to the central word without moving your eyes. You may try reading in a circular pattern, which means that if you go clockwise, you'll be reading words in reverse order at the bottom of the circle.

If you successfully do one circle—and it won't be easy at first—try moving out to a second concentric circle. Again, instead of moving your eyes, try softening your gaze. See how many circles you can complete. Take a few seconds between each one. Write down how well you were able to do in your log.

When your eye starts getting to the width of the column, see if you can perhaps read a paragraph without moving your eyes. There's no penalty if you move your eyes a little, and with time, hopefully it will stop. If this is a problem, consider using window cards.

Putting a normal window card over the text will limit your vision to that line, and you can put another card with a window that is only a few words wide over it. If you want to have someone help you, they can put the card over some words while you aren't looking, then give you a quick peek at the words. Honestly, while this is possible, it will be far more practical to use RSVP software on the computer.

Mental Grouping

Another exercise, which you can also use when you are actually reading, is to try and group the words into longer thoughts. So for instance, if you were to try and read this paragraph one word at a time, it would be formatted just the way you see it.

But if you were to read it two words at a time, it would look
like   this.   Two
words are   not much   help, though.   Maybe you   could try   moving
up   to   groups
of three.

Three-word groups   start to make   things a little   more logical. But
they   are   still
pretty artificial and   cause occasional jumps   in your thoughts.

So it makes the most sense   to try and read   in groups   that
are   full   thoughts.
This will be the fastest   and will keep comprehension   high at
the same time.

To split the line up into a fixed number of eye movements, you can put
reference marks on your tracker or pacer. This will probably require a
new pacer for each book, or at least each book that uses a different font
or size of type. It will approximate groupings of a certain number of
words, but it won't be exact.

A tool for creating spaced texts that you can use can be found on the
internet at www.superreading.com/hopify/hopify.cgi.

You can also use your hand. Typically, two or three fingers are a
reasonable-sized group, but if you want to use four, you can bend your
knuckles and use them instead of your fingertips.

For "logical groups," or those that contain a full thought, it's not possible
to make a simple pacer since there's no consistent length among
different groups of words. If you want to prepare some exercises ahead
of time, you can take any text you like and paste it into a notepad, text
editor, or word processor. Then you can reformat it however you want.

Perhaps by making several pages of text grouped by twos, several more
with text grouped by threes, and another batch with either longer groups

or logical grouping, you can provide yourself with a fair number of exercises. You can do timed trials with this material as well.

Common Phrases

In Chapter 5, it was mentioned that you can get common English phrases from websites such as www.englishspeak.com/en/english-phrases. You can also search for other sites. While this is not a comprehension exercise at all—it's actually gibberish, which can be fun—it is a good way to create exercises that use very common sets of words. You can take some of these common phrases and put them onto a page in groups to create an effective and fun practice drill, or you can use them in an RSVP program. Here is a short example:

Be careful	Don't worry	Everyone knows it
From time to time	I ate already	I think it's very good
Take a chance	Thanks for your help	On the left
See attached	What do you think?	Are you going to lunch?
Which one is the best?	They'll be right back	On the other hand
Here you are	How long will it take?	See you next week

There may be other phrases you come across frequently, so feel free to use anything you like. This is just an example to get you started.

As was mentioned before, you can see how devoting a few minutes to preparing material for your next session is an important part of your training regimen. It's more effective to work on exercises that you created some time ago so that they aren't still floating around your short-term memory, skewing your times.

But don't use your preparation as an excuse to skip practice! It's better to keep to your schedule than wait for the perfect conditions. You might also be able to get a friend or family member to do you a favor and help prepare some materials for you.

Peripheral Vision

Try tilting your head down slightly or tilting your eyeballs down a little lower than the line you are trying to read. If you have ever worn glasses and looked over the tops of them to see something, that is what it should feel like. If it's more comfortable, you can tilt your head up instead of down and look down as if you were looking down your nose. The idea is to use your peripheral vision to look at your book.

While doing this, try taking in an entire line of text at one time. You may be a little surprised at how easy it is to do with either one or no jumps of the eye. After getting comfortable, you might get a card or other tracker and try reading this way. You can combine this with sprints as well to see how well you do.

If you get good at doing this, it doesn't mean you should *only* read this way. Reading using your central vision is also useful—remember, you won't *always* be speed reading—and switching between central vision and peripheral vision is a good way to stretch your eye muscles. As with any repetitive motion, you want to break it up so that no muscle gets strained.

Pacing

When you do sprints, you try to read as fast as you can. When you do pacing drills, you read at a controlled pace, then you increase the pace.

There are several ways to practice pacing, but you will get the most benefit if you already have some grouping skills under your belt.

The first way to pace yourself is by using your tracker, whether it's your finger, the edge of a screen, or a card with a window. Turning on auto-scroll can be a great way to set the pace. You want to start at a speed that is very comfortable, then increase it a little bit to where you are keeping up but have to work at it.

It's good to do this as a timed exercise, noting your start point and how far you get before the timer expires. You can reread sections and do paced sprints, or you can keep reading from the stopping point every time. You can use material you have formatted into word groups, or you can do logical grouping in your head. You can do fixed saccades as well.

The best thing to do, though, is to regulate the tempo. There are two main ways to do that: by counting or by using a metronome. So, for example, if you split your lines into groups of three using formatting, you would set a tempo and count "one, two, three, one, two, three…" as if you were dancing the waltz. This also helps to keep you from subvocalizing. Another approach is to put three marks at equal distances along your tracking card to guide your eyes to those stopping points.

If you find that difficult or need a steadier beat, then you can use a metronome. A physical windup metronome is fine, or there are apps for smartphones and computers. The tempo should not be too fast at first. If you are trying too many techniques at once and are having a hard time keeping up, then simplify things. The important thing is to find the level you are comfortable at and start pushing from there.

Once you feel you are reading a line, then change something. Move the tempo up and try to keep up with it. When you have moved up to where you just can't keep up anymore, try reducing the tempo a few notches but also work on reducing the number of fixations. For example, if you start at 60 beats per minute (bpm) and three fixations per line and move up to 100 bpm but can't keep up, try turning it down to 80 bpm and using only two fixations per line. See if you can get up over 100 bpm now.

General Awareness

The more aware you are of things in general, the less likely it is that you're encountering something for the first time. This means that you will read it faster and comprehend it better. In a general sense, this sounds like advising you to "just know everything." Obviously we can't! But there are some specific ways that this can be put to work.

When you encounter a word you don't know, you must slow down. You have to spend time deciphering it, figuring out what it means from context clues, or the slowest thing of all: putting the book aside while you look in a dictionary. In a perfect world, you wouldn't ever come across a word you don't know. It's *not* a perfect world, but you can get closer to it by improving your vocabulary.

Building your vocabulary is a broad topic and possibly the subject for a whole book of its own. There are a few general things you can do to help build your vocabulary. Things like crossword puzzles and other word games can help. Reading new books and being curious are great ways to learn new things. Spending time with a dictionary and thesaurus to pick five words that are interesting just because you like them can also be helpful.

If you look at the front of a dictionary, you will usually find a section on prefixes, suffixes, and roots of words (Ostrov, 2002). Spend a few minutes studying this—taking these in combination will give you hundreds, if not thousands, of words. Once you understand a root, then you have keys to many words.

For example, *spec* and *spic* mean to look or see. From them, we get spectator, inspector, spectrum, speculation, conspicuous, and suspicious, among others. Being familiar with the way words are built from smaller pieces can greatly increase the size of your vocabulary.

You can use flash cards with roots, prefixes, and suffixes if that's helpful to you. You can also get or make flashcards with whole vocabulary words (*How to Improve Your Vocabulary*, 2021). There are "word of the day" websites or even desk calendars. The point is to have a constant trickle of new words into your brain.

Studying French, even more than other languages, is an excellent way to build your vocabulary. For hundreds of years after the Norman conquest in 1066, French was spoken in the medieval courts of England. The result is that about 45% of the words in the English language come from French (*Connection and Similarities*, 2021).

Similarly, general knowledge and trivia will increase the chance that some new piece of information you read will have a place in your mind where it fits neatly. Trivia games, quiz shows, and puzzles are all going to have a long-term effect on how fast you can read. In a sense, if you have the attitude that everything you are doing is part of being more alert and aware, you will be able to do everything faster and more accurately— including reading.

Using Your Library to Practice

It would be easy enough to make up practice exercises or spend money on materials for training, but the fact is that you can use things found around your house just as easily. Libraries, used bookstores, and thrift shops are full of books. There are online books from sources like Project Gutenberg (www.gutenberg.org) in addition to buying new books online or in a store. It takes very little extra work to prepare your own exercises.

When you choose a book for drills, you don't want to choose a book that is either too interesting or too boring. A dictionary or a book about plants that is just a list aren't going to work because they don't really count as structured language.

A super exciting thriller, one that you just can't put down, seems like it would be a great choice because you'd love reading it so much. But that's not always true either. You can use some juicy material from time to time, but you don't want it to be so interesting that it makes you forget the techniques you're supposed to be drilling.

Books that have a high ratio of pictures to text are also not as good a choice. You may find that older, used editions are sometimes a better value because printing photos was more expensive than it is now. An old paperback copy of *Moby Dick* might be had for a couple of dollars or even for free at the annual library book sale.

Again, for drilling, the material isn't the *most* important thing. Your best option is to find a book that has a reasonable size type and page layout. Look at potential practice materials from a visual perspective, not that of a book critic.

No, this book hasn't given you a workbook and lots of exercises that are set up for you to use right away. Instead, you have learned how to make your own training material using things found around the house. Yes, it takes a little extra time to prepare your own training, but that is time well spent because it helps reinforce that reading and training for reading require acts of devotion on your part. Making your own practice material is one of those acts.

Training Regimen

To tie things together, you should make sure that you are eating and sleeping well. Just like you would if you had a big exam or sporting event coming up, you want to be prepared mentally and physically. Make sure you practice at least once every day. You should set a goal for each practice session, a goal for the day (if you have more than one session a day), and a weekly goal.

If you miss a goal once, that's just an incentive to try harder the next time—for the same goal. But if you miss a goal three times, stop and reevaluate. You may be trying to move faster than you reasonably can. There's no "hall of shame" if you need to readjust. There's no time limit saying you must read 1,000 wpm by a certain time—that's not a goal, that's just silly.

While you can do timed exercises like sprints daily or multiple times a day, that's not the same as a good five- or 10-minute timed session once a week. And that's how often you should really check. Small variations just aren't that important. The absolute most important thing is to keep at it. As soon as you stop, you stop getting better. In 1957, when he was 80 years old, world-renowned cellist Pablo Casals was asked why he continues to practice four and five hours a day. Casals's reply was, "Because I think I am making progress" (*Because I Think*, 2021).

Summary

This chapter has given you ways to train your eyes, drills for your concentration, and even told you to study French. You have learned that you should make a distinction between when you are training for speed reading and when you are doing "real" reading.

You need to train every day, two or three times a day if you can, and keep records of what you have accomplished and where your weak spots are. That way you can see your progress and take action based on evidence when you have to. All that is left for you to do is get busy and read!

Conclusion

This is where we have to part ways. You have the tools you need to improve your reading. You have learned about your eyes and your brain, and you have some ideas about how to use them more efficiently. You know when to rest them.

You have probably learned all you need to know about how to take a behavior and turn it into a habit by making it routine and by training yourself to make routines into reflexes. You have a log of book learning, but what you need now is practice. You need to practice concentration, focus, and avoiding distractions. That's something you can only learn by doing.

If you could only remember five words from this book and had to forget all the others, what would those five words be? Before you get lost trying to remember about fixations, saccades, short-term memory, grouping, or any of the others, stop. The answer is simple.

1. Don't

2. Multitask

3. Practice

4. Every

5. Day

Refer back to Chapter 9 as you get into your practice regimen. The glossary will also help you as a quick reference. You probably won't have to reread the earlier chapters as much or as often. If you want to go out and buy other guides or practice materials, you absolutely can, but if you don't have two red cents to rub together, you can still train to achieve your peak performance.

You will find that the results you get out of speed reading are a reflection of the effort you put into it. At the same time, you may find that you have learned self-discipline and that you can profit from applying these techniques to other areas of your life.

Glossary

Attention span: The length of time a person can spend on a task before becoming distracted.

Auto-scroll: A function of a program or web browser to continuously move through the text, usually at an adjustable rate.

Backtracking: When the eyes move back over text that has already been read.

Behavioral conditioning: The process of developing automatic responses to stimuli.

Bias: Assumptions and prejudice that can color judgment and prevent objective evaluation.

Brain training: Doing mental or cognitive exercises to improve memory, processing, and other mental processes.

Central vision: The most highly focused part of the field of vision, located in the middle.

Cognitive: Being involved with or related to the mechanisms of thought.

Comprehension: The ability to understand information in the sense of cognitive processing.

Correctable vision: Eyesight that can be corrected to within normal range by glasses or contact lenses.

Cue: A prompt for a behavioral response. See *stimulus*.

Craving: The desire generated by a cue.

Decoding: The first stage of reading processing, recognizing letters and words from visual stimuli.

Disinformation: Also called "fake news," disinformation is false or partially true statements spread with the intent to deceive.

Executive function: The high-level brain functions that supervise other mental processes while a person is engaged in performing a task.

Eye fatigue: Symptoms such as tiredness, scratchiness, dryness, headache, or general fatigue that come from repetitive overuse of the eyes.

Eye span: Number of words or letters the eye can decode at one time without moving.

Fixation: When the eye stops at a letter, word, or group of words while reading.

fMRI: Functional magnetic resonance imaging. A form of noninvasive scanning that can show chemical and electrical activity in different parts of the brain while performing a task.

Functional illiteracy: When a person might have some reading skills but cannot make practical use of information they read.

Glare: Bright light that prevents seeing clearly.

Grouping: Looking at several words at a time in groups, or "chunks," to reduce the number of *fixations* and *saccades* in reading a line.

Inhibition: An executive function that sifts through information as a person reads, ignoring the bad information.

Justification: The way lines of text are formatted to be even. Full justification has even margins all the way down both sides of the page;

left-justified text is even on the left and ragged on the right but is the fastest to read.

Language comprehension: The ability to understand a language, whether written or spoken.

Long-term memory: Information that is retained long after being used in a task. The length could be from several minutes to a lifetime.

Misinformation: Information that is incorrect, the spread of which is due to ignorance of the fact, not in a premeditated way.

Multitasking: The mythical idea that a person can do more than one complex task at a time.

Neurodivergent: A term describing thought processes that are different from the statistical norm, or people who have such thought processes. They can be advantageous or disadvantageous.

Neurotypical: Thought processes that are the same as the statistical norm, or people who have such thought processes.

Pacer: A visual aid used to draw the eye and set a reading speed.

Peripheral vision: Vision outside the area of central vision. Also called "indirect vision," it covers a wider area than central vision but is less sharp.

Previewing: The strategy of becoming familiar with the structure of a piece of writing in order to make detailed reading faster and more thorough.

Reading comprehension: The product of *decoding* and *language comprehension*. Reading comprehension is a theoretical measure of how well a person learns from reading information.

Recall: The ability to retrieve information stored in memory.

Reflex: A response to a stimulus that does not require conscious thought.

Regression: *Backtracking*, or rereading something on purpose, usually because it wasn't understood.

Response (behavioral): An action taken either voluntarily or involuntarily in reaction to a stimulus.

Retention: The property of being able to recall a piece of information at a later date.

Reward: A stimulus that reinforces a response. It can be positive but could technically be negative as well.

Routine: An action or actions that are done on a regular basis at a given time.

Saccade: The jump the eyes make between *fixations*.

Short-term memory: Memory that you retain while actually doing a task. Also called "working memory."

Scanning: The process of not reading every word in a passage of text but looking for keywords, usually words that are expected.

Skimming: The process of going over passages of text reading the most important lines, either the first and last lines of a paragraph or sometimes the central lines of a paragraph, depending on the material.

Subvocalization: The "inner voice" a person hears reading words in their head.

Stimulus: An event or change, internal or external, that generates a response.

Timed reading: The process of reading for a fixed length of time, usually to measure how many words can be read.

Tracker: A visual aid used to keep the eye from *backtracking* or making *regressions*.

Working memory: See *short-term memory*.

References

Balshaw, M. (2019, May 27). *A realistic speed reading technique.* Medium. https://medium.datadriveninvestor.com/a-realistic-speed-reading-technique-a9242ffee67a

Bartels, K. (2023, January 12). *What is the best speed reading software 2023?* Speed Reading Techniques. https://www.speedreadingtechniques.org/best-speed-reading-software

Beale, A. M., & Mullan, P. (2008). *The complete idiot's guide to speed reading.* Penguin.

Because I think I am making progress. (2021, June 21). American Harp Society. https://www.harpsociety.org/news/SummFest

Benson, K. (2020, July 28). *Reading on paper versus screens: What's the difference?* Brainfacts.org. https://www.brainfacts.org/neuroscience-in-society/tech-and-the-brain/2020/reading-on-paper-versus-screens-whats-the-difference-072820

Brain-based techniques for retention of information. (2019). Loma Linda University School of Medicine. https://medicine.llu.edu/academics/resources/brain-based-techniques-retention-information

Brower, T. (2021, October 17). *Learning is a sure path to happiness: Science proves it.* Forbes. https://www.forbes.com/sites/tracybrower/2021/10/17/learning-is-a-sure-path-to-happiness-science-proves-it/?sh=3724cf4f768e

Caillet, A., Hirshberg, J., & Petti, S. (2014, December 8). *How your state of mind affects your performance.* Harvard Business Review. https://hbr.org/2014/12/how-your-state-of-mind-affects-your-performance

Cain, J. (2022, January 21). *Increase reading speed and comprehension in 5 steps.* Speed Reading Techniques. https://www.speedreadingtechniques.org/increase-reading-speed-and-comprehension

Chia, S. (2021, February 3). *15 ways to improve your focus and concentration skills.* BetterUp. https://www.betterup.com/blog/15-ways-to-improve-your-focus-and-concentration-skills

Clear, J. (2018, November 13). *How to start new habits that actually stick.* James Clear. https://jamesclear.com/three-steps-habit-change

Connection and similarities between the French and English languages. (2021, March 1). Summa Linguae. https://summalinguae.com/language-culture/know-french-english-words/

The CPD Certification Service. (2022, September 15). *Importance of repetition in learning.* The CPD Certification Service. https://cpduk.co.uk/news/importance-of-repetition-in-learning

David, S. (2012). *Brain power: How to improve your memory and speed reading techniques faster and more efficiently.* Booktango.

Edwards, P. N. (n.d.). *How to read a book* (v5.0 ed.). University of Michigan School of Information. https://pne.people.si.umich.edu/PDF/howtoread.pdf

English phrases. (n.d.). EnglishSpeak. https://www.englishspeak.com/en/english-phrases

Fezjo, R., Atkinson, L., Halmaghi, B.-G., Pagès, L.-C., & Saha, A. (2020). Improving RSVP Reading by Considering Text Complexity. *Academic Project, Human Machine Interaction.* https://doi.org/10.13140/RG.2.2.19108.91520

Flatow, I. (2013, May 10). *The myth of multitasking.* NPR. https://www.npr.org/2013/05/10/182861382/the-myth-of-multitasking

Gaid, A. (2020, December 21). *Speed reading: How to read faster before you go to sleep tonight.* Oberlo. https://www.oberlo.ca/blog/speed-reading

Habit formation. (2020, December 9). Psychology Today. https://www.psychologytoday.com/ca/basics/habit-formation

Hahn, B., Wolkenberg, F. A., Ross, T. J., Myers, C. S., Heishman, S. J., Stein, D. J., Kurup, P. K., & Stein, E. A. (2008). Divided versus selective attention: Evidence for common processing mechanisms. *Brain research, 1215,* 137–146. https://doi.org/10.1016/j.brainres.2008.03.058

Halton, M. (2019, April 1). *A speed reader shares 3 tricks to help anyone read faster.* Ideas.TED.com. https://ideas.ted.com/a-speed-reader-shares-3-tricks-to-help-anyone-read-faster/

Harvard Health Publishing. (2013, May). *Get your heart pumping in the fight against forgetfulness.* Harvard Health. https://www.health.harvard.edu/mind-and-mood/get-your-heart-pumping-in-the-fight-against-forgetfulness

Hou, J., Rashid, J., & Lee, K. M. (2017). Cognitive map or medium materiality? Reading on paper and screen. *Computers in human behavior, 67*, 84–94. https://doi.org/10.1016/j.chb.2016.10.014

How to improve your vocabulary: 7 ways to expand your vocabulary. (2021, August 3). Master Class—Articles. https://www.masterclass.com/articles/how-to-improve-your-vocabulary#6wF3lWN845m4hskbXPmXQS

IFLA. (2017, March 1). *How to spot fake news.* Internations Federation of Library Associations and Institutions. https://repository.ifla.org/handle/123456789/167

Jiban, C. (2017, December 19). *Simple, but not easy: What we forget about how reading comprehension develops.* NWEA. https://www.nwea.org/blog/2017/simple-but-not-easy-what-we-forget-about-how-reading-comprehension/

Jiban, C. (2019, September 17). *Why language matters in closing the "knowledge gap."* NWEA. https://www.nwea.org/blog/2019/why-language-matters-closing-knowledge-gap/

Keep reading to keep Alzheimer's at bay. (2014, November 12). Fisher Center for Alzheimer's Research Foundation. https://www.alzinfo.org/articles/reading-alzheimers-bay/

Kelly, J. (2023, February 8). *Council post: AI content generation won't replace humans; It will make them more powerful.* Forbes. https://www.forbes.com/sites/forbesagencycouncil/2023/02/08/ai-content-generation-wont-replace-humans-it-will-make-them-more-powerful/?sh=7c6876b772d5

Kendeou, P., van den Broek, P., Helder, A., & Karlsson, J. (2014). A cognitive view of reading comprehension: Implications for reading difficulties. *Learning disabilities research & practice, 29*(1), 10–16. https://doi.org/10.1111/ldrp.12025

King, B. (2020, January 2). *How long does it take to form a new habit?* Psychology Today. https://www.psychologytoday.com/ca/blog/taking-it-easy/202001/how-long-does-it-take-form-new-habit

Lees, S., Dayan, N., Cecotti, H., McCullagh, P., Maguire, L., Lotte, F., & Coyle, D. (2018). A review of rapid serial visual presentation-based brain–computer interfaces. *Journal of neural engineering, 15*(2), 021001. https://doi.org/10.1088/1741-2552/aa9817

Legge, G. E., Mansfield, J. Stephen., & Chung, S. T. L. (2001). Psychophysics of reading XX: Linking letter recognition to reading speed in central and peripheral vision. *Vision research, 41*(6), 725–743. https://doi.org/10.1016/s0042-6989(00)00295-9

Levinson, B. (Director). (1988). *Rain man* [Film]. MGM/UA Communications.

Mark. (2021, August 25). *Speed reading tools: A compilation of free tools.* Speed Reading Techniques. https://www.speedreadingtechniques.org/free-speed-reading-tools

Mayo Clinic. (2022a, September 15). *Eyestrain—Diagnosis and treatment.* https://www.mayoclinic.org/diseases-conditions/eyestrain/diagnosis-treatment/drc-20372403

Mayo Clinic. (2022b, September 15). *Eyestrain—Symptoms and causes.* https://www.mayoclinic.org/diseases-conditions/eyestrain/symptoms-causes/syc-20372397

Mcleod, S. (2018, October 8). *Pavlov's dogs.* Simply Psychology. https://www.simplypsychology.org/pavlov.html

Merriam-Webster. (n.d.). Devotion. In *Merriam-Webster.com dictionary.* Retrieved March 8, 2023, from https://www.merriam-webster.com/dictionary/devotion

Milkman, K. (2021, November 29). *How to build a habit in 5 steps.* CNN. https://www.cnn.com/2021/11/29/health/5-steps-habit-builder-wellness/index.html

Mozafaripour, S. (2020, May 8). *Science-backed memory tips and recall techniques.* University of St. Augustine for Health Sciences. https://www.usa.edu/blog/science-backed-memory-tips/

Napier, N. K. (2014, May 12). *The myth of multitasking.* Psychology Today. https://www.psychologytoday.com/ca/blog/creativity-without-borders/201405/the-myth-of-multitasking

Nowak, P. (2022, October 4). *Iris reading.* https://irisreading.com/skimming-vs-speed-reading-whats-the-difference/

Ostrov, R. (2002). *Power reading: The best, fastest, easiest most effective course on speed reading and comprehension ever developed!* Education Press.

Paul, C., & Matthews, M. (2016). *The Russian "Firehose of Falsehood" propaganda model: Why it might work and options to counter it.* RAND Corporation. https://doi.org/10.7249/pe198

Radford, B. (2008, May 19). *Top ten conspiracy theories.* Live Science. https://www.livescience.com/11375-top-ten-conspiracy-theories.html

Red Apple Dyslexia Association. (2021, April 30). *Eye muscles and reading.* https://dyslexiasa.org/eye-muscles-and-reading/

Rubin, G. S., & Turano, K. (1992). Reading without saccadic eye movements. *Vision research, 32*(5), 895–902. https://doi.org/10.1016/0042-6989(92)90032-e

Singer, L. M., & Alexander, P. A. (2016). Reading across mediums: Effects of reading digital and print texts on comprehension and calibration. *The journal of experimental education, 85*(1), 155–172. https://doi.org/10.1080/00220973.2016.1143794

Snyder, C. (2019, January 22). *Automatically scroll down pages in your web browser.* Help Desk Geek. https://helpdeskgeek.com/how-to/automatically-scroll-down-pages-in-your-web-browser/

Speed reading methods for computer screens. (2010, August 9). Spreeder. https://www.spreeder.com/speed-reading-methods-for-computer-screen/

Speed reading on screens and digital devices. (2021). The Mind Mapping Expert. https://thespeedreadingblog.com/post/speed-reading-on-screens-and-digital-devices

Taylor, R. (2022, July 29). *5 tips to prevent eye strain while reading.* Atlantic Eye Institute. https://atlanticeyeinstitute.com/5-tips-to-prevent-eye-strain-while-reading/

Troester, A. (2023). *Tips for reading more quickly.* AJE. https://www.aje.com/en/arc/tips-for-reading-more-quickly/

University of Chicago. (2018, March 17). *The speed reading method.* The University of Chicago. https://web.archive.org/web/20180317214346/http:/wellness.uchicago.edu/page/speed-reading-method

Vanderlinde, W. (2018, July 1). *Speed reading: Fact or fiction?* Skeptical Inquirer. https://skepticalinquirer.org/2018/07/speed-reading-fact-or-fiction/

Voltaire. (1877). *Contes en Vers: Vol. Tome 10* (pp. 50–56). Garnier. https://fr.wikisource.org/wiki/Contes_en_vers_(Voltaire)/La_B%C3%A9gueule#

Wylie, A. (2021, July 30). *What's the average time spent reading [statistics!]?* Wylie Communications, Inc. https://www.wyliecomm.com/2021/07/whats-the-average-time-spent-reading-statistics/

Yu, D., Legge, G. E., Wagoner, G., & Chung, S. T. L. (2018). Training peripheral vision to read: boosting the speed of letter processing. *Vision research, 152,* 51–60. https://doi.org/10.1016/j.visres.2017.06.005

Made in the USA
Columbia, SC
29 November 2024

47912961R00070